CENSORSHIP
ALERT

I0116828

Copyright © Peter de Haan
Book design Edwin Smet

ISBN 978-90-823641-6-3

www.evatasfoundation.com

CENSORSHIP ALERT
PETER DE HAAN

CENSORSHIP
IN ECONOMICS

EVATASFOUNDATION

Amsterdam 2016

TABLE OF CONTENTS

FOREWORD

The content of this essay, part of our Foundation's Censorship series, suggests that one should worry about censorship. And – indeed – one should, as censorship is increasing in the world. Literally every day there are reports in the media about journalists, bloggers, writers, and their publishers being harassed, detained, expelled, or even killed.

There are several reasons that explain why increasing numbers of journalists, bloggers, and writers aren't able to publish their work as they please. Governments play an important part in limiting or even ending the freedom of expression. Censorship is being tightened through laws that are enacted to smother the freedom of the media, acting as a perverse means to protect the political and economic interests of those in power.

But government is not the only actor that makes the professional lives of journalists, bloggers, and writers difficult. Economic interests also impinge upon the freedom of expression: rich media tycoons with strong political connections make sure that only 'depoliticized' news is being published that serves their and those of their political friends. Religious fanatics, including al-Qaeda and Islamic State extremists, attempt to undermine freedom of expression, as demonstrated by the brutal killing of *Charlie Hebdo's* editors and cartoonists last year in Paris.

There is also the tendency to apply more and more self-censorship, triggered by the fear of losing one's job, being harassed, or of being blamed for not reporting in a politically correct fashion.

While most publications about censorship zoom in on political, ethical, and human rights aspects, this essay is also about the relationship between censorship and economic development. The author analysed how notorious 'censorship countries' fared in economic terms during the past three decades. He investigated whether censorship negatively affects the economic performance of countries. In other words, do 'censorship countries' score poorly in terms of economic development? They do, and this should alert not only those involved in defending the freedom of expression but also those involved in development aid.

This essay ends as follows: 'Given the current growing threats to freedom, it is essential that all organisations dedicated to defending freedom of expression and freedom of the media must be heard loud and clear. They must strive for full cooperation with each other to enhance their impact in every country where censorship is a common phenomenon'.

The Eva Tas Foundation is prepared to take up the challenge and play its part. We will take initiatives – such as the promotion of seminars – to join hands with like-minded organisations in response to the censorship alert, as elaborated in this essay.

Rudolf Geel
Chairman Eva Tas Foundation

INTRODUCTION

This essay is written for all those who take an interest in freedom of expression and in the freedom of media in particular. It is a call to action since these freedoms, as Eva Tas Foundation's chairman noted, are increasingly under threat.

The first chapter describes the downward trend in freedom of the press and includes examples of censorship and what it affected the victims.

Chapter II is about censorship and economic development and how the two phenomena are connected. This chapter also highlights what economists, writers, and philosophers say about growth and development, as well as the positive role played by culture and literature in a society's development.

Chapter III provides a fairly comprehensive overview of organisations involved in the defence of the freedom of expression and freedom of the media. It is particularly helpful for journalists, bloggers, and writers who are under threat or need help. The central message of this chapter is that there are organisations out there that can help. In addition, it is a useful overview for those who want to take action against censorship, but do want to do so together with others.

Chapter IV draws some conclusions and ends with a call for collective action.

Annexe I includes Freedom House's methodology. Annexe II presents the dot plots and the statistical details of the regression analyses as presented in Chapter II.

A bibliography and a list of the foundation's censorship publications are provided at end of this booklet.

ACKNOWLEDGEMENTS

I am indebted to Dr. Marein van Schaaijk, Director of Micro-Macro Consultants, who agreed have the regression analyses undertaken by his junior partner, Sibren Vegter, who did a sterling job.

The inspiring discussion with Sophie Leferink of HIVOS, a Dutch funding organisation, helped me a lot in conceptualising this essay.

Simone Whittemore improved my English to the extent that – I hope and trust – it can't be distinguished from a text written by a native speaker. The many high-flying discussions I had with Eva Tas Foundation Board member Jan Honout, gave me much advice and inspiration, in particular in the elaboration of the economic development dimension of censorship. My thanks to him are, therefore, heartfelt indeed.

This also goes for the Board of the Eva Tas Foundation who gave me the opportunity and the trust to write this essay.

Peter de Haan
December 2015

CHAPTER I

CENSORSHIP TRENDS OVER THE PERIOD 2006-2015

'Everyone has the right to freedom of opinion and expression; this right includes freedom to hold opinions without interference and to seek, receive, and impart information and ideas through any media regardless of frontiers'.

Article 19 of the Universal Declaration of Human Rights (UDHR), cited above, commits all states to everyone's right of freedom of expression. But do the countries that signed up to the Declaration live up to its contents? The answer is that some do, but an increasing number of countries don't. This chapter describes trends and the fate of censorship's prime victims.

_ 2006

Trends

Freedom House's *Global Press Freedom Report* 2007 noted that the state of global press freedom declined in 2006, with worrisome trends in Asia, the former Soviet Union, and Latin America. Surely, there were improvements in some countries, but these were eclipsed by the worsening situation in others. Of 195 countries and territories assessed, 74 countries were rated 'Free', 58 were rated 'Partly Free', and 63 were rated 'Not Free'. Only 18% of the world's population lived in countries that enjoyed a free press. ¹he decline in media freedom was the more regrettable as media freedom had made gains during the 1980s and early 1990s. This inspiring development, however, stalled when, during the second half of the 1990s a decade of media stagnation ensued in line with a pattern of stagnation in political freedom.

Causes

The *Global Press Freedom Report* 2007 identified four main causes for the worsening media environment worldwide. The reversal of political freedom in e.g., Russia, Venezuela, and Zimbabwe, was responsible for cracking

---

1 The 'Not Free' and the 'Partly Free' categories are influenced by China, with a 'Not Free' rating, and India, with a 'Partly Free' rating, which together account for 1/3 of the world's population.

down on the media. Political upheaval in the form of coups and states of emergency was a second cause. The media in Bangladesh, Pakistan, Sri Lanka, the Philippines, Thailand, and Fiji all suffered setbacks.

The third cause for this worsening trend was the increase in violence against journalists. Who doesn't remember the assassination of Russian journalist Anna Politkovskaya in 2006? [2] But she wasn't the only one. Mexican and Columbian reporters were killed by drug gangs. And in Iraq, Pakistan, Sri Lanka, and the Philippines journalists were killed for doing their job.

Cause number four involved the application of laws prohibiting blasphemy, hate speech, and endangering the national security. These laws used to be applied by Middle Eastern governments in particular, but gained popularity, so to speak, in some Asian, African, and former Soviet Union countries as well. The 2007 report specifically mentioned Turkey where 293 writers and journalists were persecuted under Article 301 of Turkey's revised penal code, which prohibits denigrating 'Turkishness'.

Positive developments
There were not only negative trends; on the positive side, Italy regained its 'Free' status after the exit of Prime Minister Silvio Berlusconi. Colombia, Haiti, Indonesia, Macedonia, and Nepal improved their scores as well. Press freedom scores of quite a few Sub-Saharan African countries – such as Angola, the Central African Republic, Cape Verde, Mozambique, and Sudan – also improved.

Worst of the worst
In 2006 according to Freedom House the Worst of the worst-rated countries were: Burma, Cuba, Libya, North Korea, and Turkmenistan, followed by Belarus, Uzbekistan, Equatorial Guinea, Eritrea, and Zimbabwe. [3]

---

2 Anna Politkovskaya received assistance from the PEN Emergency Fund, as elaborated in Chapter III, the section about the PEN Emergency Fund.
3 This list is identical to CPJ's 2006 list (presented in Chapter II) with the exception of Zimbabwe. In its place CPJ included Syria.

The Internet
The *Global Press Freedom Report* 2007 paid special attention to the restrictions on the Internet:

The internet has emerged as one of the most potent weapons against censorship and lack of transparency in authoritarian societies. Even in China and Iran, where the authorities have devoted significant resources to the control of internet content, internet-based outlets have remained a vital source of news about social upheaval, labor disputes, official corruption, and acts of state abuse against the citizenry. [4]

China, Vietnam, and Iran all controlled access to the Internet. These countries imprisoned journalists and 'cyber dissidents' who filed unwelcome reports. Ethiopia, and The Gambia imposed controls on bloggers and websites, despite low levels of internet penetration in them.

_ 2015
In 2006 the trend in media freedom compared unfavorably with the early 1990s, but it became worse after that year. This may well have coincided with the slowing down – if not reversal – of the democratisation process throughout the world, as explained in chapter II.

The 2015 *Global Press Freedom Report* observed that conditions for the media had deteriorated sharply. Journalists around the world faced mounting restrictions on the free flow of news and information. Some feared for their lives and fled their countries, others were killed. The *Committee to Protect Journalists* (CPJ) reported an increasing trend in journalists being killed since the beginning of the 21st century. Terrorists and criminal elements kidnapped, and in some cases even murdered, journalists who tried to report on armed conflicts. A sad and brutal reminder: freelance journalists James Foley and Steven Sotloff were beheaded by IS-militants in 2014.

---

4 *Global Press Freedom Report* 2007, p. 4.

Number of journalists killed

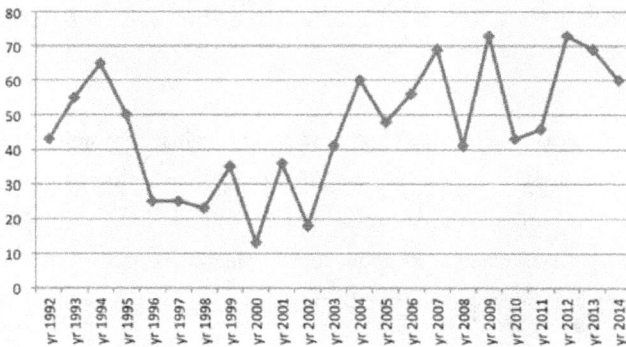

Source: *Global Press Freedom Report 2015*

Of the 1,135 journalists killed since 1992 by CPJ's count, 36% died during armed conflict, while 44% covered politics. Another 20% were investigating corruption, 18% worked on human rights abuses, and 15% on crime. [5] This sobering number did not include the 93 media workers who lost their lives as well. Under the heading 'motive unconfirmed' another 436 journalists and media workers were included in CPJ's list. [6]

 Regarding the armed conflict in Syria, Emma Daly, Director Communications of *Human Rights Watch*, wrote in *Why we need journalism*, how the war in Syria makes independent journalism near impossible and how literally killing it is for journalists, including citizen journalists, to report from there.

Since World Press Freedom Day in 2013, at least 60 journalists have been killed because of their work, with Syria and Iraq as the most dangerous places. Of course Syrian journalists are at greatest risk– including the many "citizen journalists" and activists working to get information out about the fighting. International reporters have shown themselves willing to take the risks normally associated with covering conflict, but the very direct threats of kidnap have prompted many news organizations to reduce or end coverage inside Syria. In December, more than a dozen international media companies

---

5 Some covered more than one beat.
6 When the motive is unclear, but it is possible that a journalist was killed because of his or her work, CPJ classifies the case as "unconfirmed" and continues to investigate.

wrote to the Supreme Military Council (SMC) of the opposition Free Syrian Army about the "increasingly common risk of abduction." Because of the increased threat, they wrote, many outlets "have decided to limit their coverage of the war." In response, the SMC promised to protect and support journalists, but said that most potential kidnappers were outside their control. Media workers, including citizen journalists, are also being targeted by government forces and pro-government militias. Many have been arrested and detained arbitrarily, tortured or disappeared. More than 50 journalists have been killed during the three years of conflict because of their work, and at least 70 experienced Syrian journalists are reported to have fled the country. [7]

Trend

The Global Press Freedom Report 2015 underscored that in 2014 global press freedom dropped to its lowest point in more than a decade. Worse, the decline accelerated dramatically, with the global average score suffering its largest one-year decline in ten years.

In 2014 there were 63 countries enjoying a free press. That is 14% in terms of the world's population; the equivalent of one in seven people. The percentage of those enjoying a 'Free' media in 2014 was at its lowest level since 1996 when Freedom House (FH) started incorporating population figures. Three times more people (42% of the world's population) lived in 71 'Partly Free' countries. And 44% of the world's population lived in 65 'Not Free' countries or territories.

The 2015 report concluded that all regions – except Sub-Saharan Africa whose average score improved slightly – experienced declines of varying degrees, with the Middle East and North Africa showing the largest net decline.

Causes

The report presented two factors for the decline: (i) the passage and use of restrictive laws against the press (often on national security grounds) to protect the interests of the power holders; and, (ii) the inability of local and foreign journalists to access and report freely from a given country.

The report rightly noted that – paradoxically – in a time of almost unlimited

7 Daly, E. We Need Journalism. Esglbal.org (2 May 2014).

access to information, and new methods of content delivery, more and more areas of the world are becoming virtually inaccessible, such as China's Tibet and Xinjiang regions, Russian-occupied Crimea, and ethnic minority areas in Myanmar. IS-affiliated Boko Haram-controlled areas in Nigeria and the Sinaï peninsula were off-limits for journalists as well.

FH also reported that access to the internet declined in 2014. China is censoring the internet most of all countries, followed by Syria and Iran. Almost half of all internet users live in countries where people have been harassed or even killed for using the internet.

Examples

In Latin American countries, such as Mexico and Honduras (as described in the box below), violence against journalists soared in 2104. Local governments and gangs successfully blocked reporting on drugs-related crime and corruption. According to Mexican journalist Carmen Aristegui, colleagues of her working in the provinces encounter great difficulties reporting the facts about shady activities of drug cartels. Since 2000 89 journalists have been killed in Mexico. These journalists didn't enjoy the international protection Ms. Aristegui enjoys. [8]

'However, at the same time, the state has armed itself with its apparatus of repression to subdue them and to protect the interests of economic groups. Everything functions in a coordinated way. This elite has at its disposal most of the media which distorts information and makes it appear that the elite is working for the public good. The justice system is no different and acts to protect those interests through the criminalization of social movements, journalists and other sectors of the population. The truth about all this remains kidnapped in the newsroom. The public does not have access to information and that gives more power to this elite that not only uses censorship but also kills those who are vocal in their criticism'.

From: *Kidnapped*, by Dina Meza. Amsterdam: Eva Tas Foundation (2015).

---

[8] Interview in NRC Handelsblad, 17 November 2015, p. C2.

Citizen journalists and ordinary citizens managed to send some information out about the conditions in these regions, but this is not the same as professional reporting by seasoned journalists.

'On January 17, authorities arrested Solomon Kebede, columnist and managing editor of *Muslim Affairs*. They charged him along with 27 other Muslims in April under the anti-terrorist proclamation.... Basically, prosecutors use documents of government criticism as evidence against journalists, bloggers, and dissenting politicians. Several opposition political leaders (mainly young politicians), are also imprisoned accused of or charged with terrorism and other grave crimes. Almost all journalists, bloggers, and politicians mentioned above are victims of the Anti-Terrorism Law of the country. The charges are indicative of the Ethiopian government's way of misusing this law to smother free speech and the functioning of free media'.
From: *Censorship is the Genocide of Thought*, by exiled Ethiopian journalist Bisrat Woldemichael Handiso. Amsterdam: Eva Tas Foundation (2015).

Other countries cracked down on freedom of expression and the media as well.[9] Thailand's military rulers suspended the constitution and imposed martial law while shutting down media outlets. Turkey's intelligence organisation exerted its surveillance of almost all information held by any entity in the country.

The Russian legislature passed a law allowing the authorities to apply new controls on blogs and social media. Azerbaijan detained nine journalists under the guise of security or emergency laws; some media advocacy groups there were forced to fold as well.

On 28 May 2013 police knocked on Tomislav Kezharovski's door, founder of the independent Macedonian magazine *Reporter 92*. He was sentenced to four –and-a-half years imprisonment for writing the truth about what is happening in Macedonia. Thanks to widespread international protests he was released after two years. This is what he wrote about his motives to start *Reporter 92*:

---

9 Most examples below are taken from the 2015 *Global Press Freedom Report*.

It was to be a publication where I would criticize all that was not right, where mistakes would be pointed out and where no one would be spared. I wanted to create something of value, of substance. I believed I could; I believed that I would succeed.... Not even in my wildest dreams could I imagine the attacks over my body and work. I've had to face the cruel truth, the fact that I can never again live a normal life in Macedonia'. [10]

South African authorities expanded their *National Key Points Act* (a relic from the Apartheid era) to prevent investigative journalists from reporting on important sites or institutions. *The Economist* reported in its 27th June 2015 issue that President Zuma had urged all media to be more 'patriotic', while his government uses taxpayers' money to bolster private media that sing the ruling party's praises. A senior manager at the South African Broadcasting Corporation had reportedly demanded a 70% 'happy news' quota.

In Egypt, three Al-Jazeera journalists were sentenced to three years in prison for allegedly conspiring with the outlawed Muslim Brotherhood to broadcast false reports. The good news is that Ahmed Mansoor, another Al -Jazeera journalist convicted in absentia by the Egyptian judiciary, had travelled to Germany where he was erroneously arrested by the German police. However, after having realized their mistake, the German authorities set him free.

Saudi Arabia intends to continue the lashing of Saudi blogger Raif Badawi, once the Supreme Court has decided on his case. Badawi had already received 50 lashings pending the verdict. Badawi established the website *Saudi Liberal Network* in 2012. He was awarded the 2015 European Parliament's Sacharov Prize. *Amnesty International* posted a full-page advertisement in newspapers to draw attention to the case. The most recent PEN International Congress held in Montreal, Canada, paid due attention to his case as well. Censorship was also applied by states that in the past did not belong to the notorious group of censorship countries. For example, Greece's public broadcasting company had to counter allegations of political interference in hiring staff. And in Hungary, the Orbán administration exerted pressure on media owners to report favourably on the government's actions. Newspapers that reported critically were harassed.

10 Kezharovski, T. (2015) *Annihilation/Likvidacija*. Amsterdam: Eva Tas Foundation, p. 8.

Table I: Country Classification: Free, Partly Free, Not Free 2006-2014

Year	Free Press countries	Partly Free Press countries	Not Free Press countries	% of world's inhabitants enjoying free press
2006	74	58	63	18%
2014	63	71	65	14%

Source: *Global Press Freedom Reports 2007 and 2015*

Writers' freedom, independence, and political engagement
So far, censorship has been analysed in the context of reporting, of journalism in general. Obviously, writers also suffer from censorship. When confronted with censorship they cannot publish what they want to express in their work. In particular PEN International, the global association of poets, playwrights, editors, essayists, and novelists, defends their freedom of expression, whenever and wherever needed. The PEN tries to stay away from political interference. This hasn't always been easy. After all, writers play an important role in the public debate about political and moral issues of the societies they belong to.

Thomas von Vegesack argues that writers belong to the intellectual class in any society; writers are public personalities.[11] He presents a compelling historical account of how intellectuals were judged by public opinion from the Dreyfus affair of 1898 up to the May 1968 rebellion in Paris. The author explains how writers, often members of PEN International, struggled with finding a balance between their independence and their political convictions, while criticizing the authorities.

Intellectuals didn't always have a good reputation. For example, the famous economist Joseph Schumpeter argued that intellectuals are people

---

11 Thomas von Vegesack provides a detailed account of the threats to PEN's independence in *Tankens aristokrater eller pannans betjänter* (1986). His book was translated in Dutch entitled: *De Intellectuelen; een geschiedenis van het literaire engagement 1898-1968*. Amsterdam: Meulenhoff (1989).

who wield the power of the spoken and written word. One of the most significant areas that distinguish them from other people is the absence of direct responsibility for practical affairs; they only have a 'nuisance value'.[12] Others had a higher opinion of the role played by intellectuals. The German author Gottfried Benn, for example, argued that a society develops thanks to its natural intellectual force.

Freedom of expression and independence are terms that the writers, portrayed in Von Vegesack's book, often use. For example, French author André Gide, who struggled with his initial admiration for the Soviet Union, wrote that without freedom art loses its relevance and value. Vegesack also refers to George Orwell's essay *Inside the Whale* about the independence of writers:

For any writer who accepts ....the discipline of a political party is sooner or later faced with the alternative: toe the line, or shut up. It is, of course, possible to toe the line and go on writing... Any Marxist can demonstrate... that 'bourgeois' liberty of thought is an illusion. But when he has finished his demonstration there remains the psychological fact that without this bourgeois liberty the creative powers wither away.[13]

Orwell had more to say about censorship and literature. He once attended a PEN Club meeting in London in defence of the freedom of expression. There was a panel of four speakers. One of the panel members defended the Russian *purges* which had taken place under Stalin, but no one in the audience mentioned political liberty and no one mentioned press freedom. Orwell added that if political liberty and press freedom were to mean anything at all, it would mean having the freedom to oppose and criticize. Orwell wrote an essay inspired by this PEN Club meeting entitled *The Prevention of Literature*. [14] In it he says a few memorable things: the writer is unfree when he has to falsify his subjective feelings, which from his point of view are facts; he cannot say with any conviction that he likes what he

---

12 Schumpeter, J.A. (1970) *Capitalism, Socialism and Democracy*. London: Unwin University Books, p.147.
13 Orwell, G. (1984) The Penguin Essays of George Orwell, *Inside the Whale*. Harmondsworth: Penguin Books.
14 Ibid., *The Prevention of Literature*, p.335

dislikes. The only thing which is of value to the writer is his freedom of expression and literature is doomed if liberty of thought is under threat. Orwell ended the essay as follows:

At present we know only that the imagination, like certain wild animals, will not breed in captivity. And writer or journalist who denies that fact ….is, in effect, demanding his own destruction. [15]

Vegesack devotes an entire chapter to the growing ideological distance between Albert Camus and Jean Paul Sartre which began in 1951.[16] Initially, these two great French writers shared similar political views. Sartre regularly visited the Soviet Union, where he was given the VIP treatment. He maintained his sympathies for communism well into old age. Camus, in contrast, was no *fellow-traveller*; he was an 'unpolitical man'. [17] Vegesack observed that those who – like Sartre – have strong beliefs in the course of history, can share the opinion that killing people to ensure a better future for all is necessary and unavoidable. But those who – like Camus – believe that the value of happiness is the same for any *person*, would find that killing people for a possible better future is a horrible and unacceptable sacrifice. Camus was a writer and a *moralist*. Camus took a balanced view and – like Orwell – didn't close his eyes to the atrocities committed in communist countries. This didn't go down well in the left-leaning politicized Parisian ambiance. Camus became silent on political issues but continued to point out the moral dimension of the issues at hand.

Vegesack ends his book by quoting the French philosopher Roland Barthes, who made a distinction between an author and a 'scribent'. The author is limited by the structure of the language and not by anything else. The scribent is someone who is not only applying the structure of the language but also this 'anything else', which is political engagement. A scribent is someone who, whenever there is an opportunity, shares his

---

15 Ibid., p. 346.
16 In that year Camus published L'Homme révolté, which is about the idea of man in revolt, and represents a direct attack on the revolutionary myth that was reflective of radical thought at the time, including the indifference to the human costs of radical political choices..
17 This is Tony Judt's characterization of Camus in his essay: Albert Camus: The Reluctant Moralist. In: The Burden of Responsibility. Chicago: Chicago University Press, 1998.

(political) opinion with a wider audience. The story about Sartre and Camus does in fact illustrate Barthes's distinction: Camus the author and Sartre the scribent.

Being public personalities, writers sometimes cannot escape from making statements which implicitly or explicitly are political in nature. However, their central issue is to defend the freedom of expression, without which they either can't work or have to compromise their independence as a writer.

Trend

PEN's *Writers in Prison Committee* (WiPC) publishes an annual *case list* of imprisoned writers, and of writers who have been killed, tortured, or molested by other means. The PEN Emergency Fund financially assists some of victims.

'The power of one is hope; the power of many is change. I believe that as individuals we are all entitled to have hopes and dreams. No dictatorship ever succeeds in killing the people's aspirations. However, as individuals, by acting alone we lack a collective force necessary to bring about the changes we hope for. International PEN and its affiliation, the PEN Emergency Fund and the OxfamNovib PEN-award in particular, have helped to bring about joint forces from hundreds of Vietnamese writers to millions of other fellow defenders of free expression around the world. Together we create a collective power for freedom of expression to prevail. In that collectiveness, today in honour of my fallen writers and those who are still languishing in prisons and all those who have given me the privilege to stand with them in the line of duty for defence of human rights and for those who are forbidden by the Vietnamese authorities to stand with me here today, I'd like to accept this prestigious award on their behalf'. Part of the acceptance speech of Christine Dang, winner of the OxfamNovib PEN-award 2009. From: PEN *Emergency Fund Fundraising flyer*.

The PEN Emergency Fund has assisted writers, poets and essayists such as Aung San Suu Kyi, Josef Brodsky, Maria Elena Cruz Varela, Salman Rushdie, Ken Saro-Wiwa, Anna Politkovskaya, Hrant Dink, and Nobel Peace Prize laureate, Liu Xiaobo. Some of this assistance was successful, such as the release of Iranian writer Faraj Sarkohi. However, others ended in tragedy, such as the hanging of the Nigerian writer Ken Saro-Wiwa, who defended the plight of the Ogoni people and brought to attention the environmental damage caused by huge oil spills.

A comparison of the case lists is presented for the years 2006 and 2015 to show what the trend is in terms of imprisoned, harassed, or killed writers.

_ 2006

2006 was a turbulent year for writers and journalists. The Danish anti-Islam extremist cartoons uproar, which flared up at the end of 2005, spilled over into early 2006. The cartoonist and the editor of *Jyllands Posten*, a Danish newspaper that ran the cartoons, received death threats. In October 2006, Russian journalist Anna Politkovskaya was murdered. In the same year Turkish novelist and Nobel laureate Orhan Pamuk was tried for insulting the Turkish state on account of his writing about the mass killings of Armenians in the beginning of the 20th century. Pamuk was acquitted, arguably thanks to international pressure and thanks to English PEN's WiPC chair, Joan Smith, who was present during the trial. However, this brief victory was overshadowed by the brutal killing on 17 January 2007 of journalist Hrant Dink.[18]

WiPC's report for 2006 noted that Aung San Suu Kyi was the longest serving detained writer under house arrest in the Committee's history. Now that she has won the 2015 parliamentary elections in Myanmar, one might conclude that the freedom of writers has improved since 2006, also taking into consideration that 64 writers in other countries were released in 2014. True, the WiPC registered more releases since 2006, but the situation now is not better than it was in 2006.

WiPC's 2006 report states that over 1,000 cases of attacks against

---

18 Hrant Dink was assisted by the PEN Emergency Fund, as mentioned in Chapter III, the section about PEN's Emergency Fund.

freedom of expression were monitored. [19]. 47 writers were killed; another 144 were serving terms clearly violating their right to freedom of expression, while 50 other cases were still under investigation.

The report observed that, while these figures remained comparable with 2005, the number of people on trial for their writings had risen by half from 148 in 2005 to 227 in 2006.

_ 2015

In contrast to the data collected by FH and CPJ over the period 2006 -2015 (see chapter II), WiPC's figures do not show an increase in harassment, imprisonment and killing of writers. As noted, WiPC's 2006 report registered 1,000 cases of 'attacks against the freedom of expression', as the report put it. WiPC's 2015 report mentions 904 cases documented during 2014. In total, 86 writers were killed, 325 were imprisoned or detained, 192 were on trial, 186 were harassed, 16 disappeared, 51 were attacked or ill-treated, 24 received death threats, four were abducted, 23 were sentenced, 38 were conditionally released, while another 64 writers were unconditionally released. These are just the data, but behind these figures are writers who not only were barred from doing their work, but were severely punished. The 1,000 cases documented by WiPC in 2006 compared to the 904 cases in 2014, doesn't mean that freedom of expression for writers has improved since 2006. The difference between the FH and CPJ data (which reflected a dramatic increase from 2006 to 2015) and those of WiPC may well be explained by the fact that the former two organisations were able to register more violations of the rights of journalists than WiPC could.

One of the reasons for the difference could well be that, in particular, FH is a better endowed organisation than most others, and therefore it can invest more widely in research and data collection.

---

19 It is not clear whether these attacks were undertaken against novelists, poets or essayists only. WiPC includes journalists as well in their data. I assume that the majority of the cases registered by WiPC concern the former group.

'For those of us involved in PEN for many years it is irresistible to look back, and to reflect on the recent history of PEN, but also, crucially, to look forward to 2021, which will mark the 100th anniversary of PEN International.

What is most significant to me, after six years as WiPC Chair, is how our work on freedom of expression has changed, not only in the past six years, but also since the early days of PEN, and specifically since the WiPC was formed in 1960, 55 years ago. The WiPC has been the leader in work on behalf of imprisoned and threatened writers. The hallmark PEN work – the naming of names, the letter-writing to prisoners, the championing of a single oppressed writer – has not only been the foundation of our own case work, a programme of action on behalf of some 25 writers in 1960, now the basis of our work on more than nine hundred cases, but has also inspired and informed the work of organizations formed after 1960, such as Amnesty International.

The main components of PEN's WiPC campaigns have consistently been the Rapid Action alerts, Congress resolutions, the adoption of (main case) imprisoned writers as honorary members by Centres, and more recently, country and region-specific campaigns, as in Turkey, China and Latin America.

PEN has led the way historically on advocacy for threatened and imprisoned individuals, and our case list has become a signature resource in the greatly expanded network of organizations working on freedom of expression.' Part of PiWC Chair's Notebook, delivered by Marian Botsford Fraser on 15 October, 2015, Quebec, Canada.

Another explanation for the difference between FH's and CPJ's data and those of WiPC would be that harassment of writers, journalists, and bloggers, often including their publishers, is now being committed in countries which in the past didn't belong to the ones that obstructed freedom of expression, and where WiPC was not well represented. Take Bangladesh, which is now regularly in the news because of the lynching of publishers such as Faisal Rashid Tutul and blogger Avjit Roy. Their brutal killings were claimed by al-Queda.

CHAPTER II
CENSORSHIP AND ECONOMIC DEVELOPMENT

There is no *causal* relationship between censorship and economic growth, as there are obviously more factors in play that explain economic growth. There are countries that limit freedom of speech and freedom of the media and yet achieve economic growth. Take China – the country registered phenomenal growth figures until recently; while the regime strictly limits freedom of the media. Neither is there a causal relationship between censorship and economic development. Singapore, for example, has one of the world's highest per capita incomes and scores very well in health and education terms; still the city-state tightly restricts free speech.

The question remains, however, whether there is some sort of relationship between censorship and economic growth, and between censorship and economic development? Before answering this question it is necessary to explain the difference between economic growth and economic development.

Economic growth and economic development
Economic growth is measured by the percentage by which a country's annual Gross Domestic Product (GDP) grows. Economic development involves more than economic growth. It is manifested by an increase in per capita income of every citizen. It includes a country's increase in living standards, improvement in self-esteem, needs, and freedom from oppression, including freedom of expression and freedom of the media. Economic development leads to the creation of more opportunities in the sectors of education, healthcare, employment, and environmental concerns. Economic growth is a necessary but not a sufficient condition for economic development. In other words, there can be economic growth that doesn't

necessarily contribute to economic development. When the benefits of growth are invested, e.g., in infrastructure, productive capital, education, health, you name it, a society transforms economic growth into economic development. [20]

Take Ethiopia: the World Bank reported that the Ethiopian economy grew 9.9% in 2014. However, more than 76 million Ethiopians still are poor. Another indication that growth and development don't necessarily function in tandem, is Ethiopia's position on the Human Development Index (HDI) list, which measures the level of development rather than only economic growth. The 2013 HDI list included 187 countries. Ethiopia is number 173 on the HDI list; a very low score. The Ethiopian political leadership's focus was apparently on economic growth, and not also on economic development.

Development creates the opportunity to fulfil basic needs so that citizens can enjoy a productive and healthy life. Positive socio-political and economic change brings a country prosperity and well-being. However, for this change to happen, both the commitment of the political leaders and transparent and participatory development policies are important.

Mature economies have demonstrated that this change can be achieved. Countries that assured economic development have fulfilled the basic needs of their people, provided good housing, adequate health care, education, and social protection in an environment where freedom of expression is ensured. How this is done depends upon historical, political, and cultural factors; there is no uniform answer available to the 'how' question.

What scholars say about development
Some scholars argue that it is industrial capitalism combined with political democracy that creates economic development. The sociologist Peter Berger is one such scholar. In *The Capitalist Revolution; Fifty Propositions about*

---

20 The *Hartwick Rule* applies to resource-rich countries. It says that all the money a country takes out of the soil (gas, oil, diamonds) should be reinvested. Dutch economist Rick van der Ploeg observed: 'Imagine if Nigeria or Venezuela would have invested its resource rents. They would have had an enormous increase in productive capital, an increase of four times'. Quote from: *Economic Growth and the Common Good*. Amsterdam: KIT Publishers, p. 46/7.

Prosperity, Equality, &Liberty (1986), Berger writes that through the interaction of economic and political forces, Western societies have progressively removed traditional barriers to the advancement of individuals regardless of their social origin. Whenever industrial capitalism is combined with political democracy, says Berger, the openness of the class system has invariably increased by giving greater access to education to people of the less privileged classes. Berger pointed out that democracy developed precisely in those Western countries in which modern capitalism unfolded. Yet, Berger warns that capitalism and democracy may not inevitably further develop in tandem, as there are built-in forces which may undermine both capitalism and democracy.

Berger alluded to the relevance of the removal of barriers to the advancement of individuals, to openness, and to the reinforcing interplay between a capitalist system and democracy.

Other researchers have come to comparable conclusions in their analysis of the factors promoting economic development. For example, development economist William Easterly maintains that all development, including economic development, is innovation. [21] If we knew how to achieve development, says Easterly, we would already be developed, but we have to invent new answers as we go along. Innovation happens because there are dissenters who dissent from the prevailing conventional wisdom. *Individual freedom and democracy* promote this social process of inventing new answers. Easterly took his insight from libertarian economist Friedrich Hayek who said: 'The interaction of individuals possessing different knowledge and different views is what constitutes the life of thought. The growth of reason is a social process based on the existence of such differences'. [22] Hayek then wondered why it is that we do not know how to achieve development: 'It is of its essence that the results of this individual freedom cannot be predicted, that we cannot know which views will assist the growth, and which will not. In short, this growth cannot be governed by any views which we now possess, without at the same time limiting it'. [23] In his monumental work

---

21 Easterly, W. (2008) Freedom and Development. In: *Democracy and Development*. Amsterdam: KIT Publishers, pp.57 – 69.
22 Ibid., p. 59.
23 Ibid., 59.

The *Constitution of Liberty*, Hayek wrote that the advance of knowledge is likely to be fastest where scientific pursuits are not determined by some unified conception of their social utility, and where each man can devote himself to the tasks in which he sees the best chance of making a contribution to the advancement of knowledge, which in turn contributes to development. The philosopher Karl Popper warned against the consequences of the suppression of reason and truth in *The Open Society and its Enemies*:

For those who have eaten of the tree of knowledge, paradise is lost. The more we try to return to the heroic age of tribalism, the more surely do we arrive at the Inquisition, at the Secret Police, and at a romanticized gangsterism. Beginning with the suppression of reason and truth, we must end with the most brutal and violent destruction of all that is human. [24]

Milton Friedman, a libertarian economist like Hayek, underscored the importance of political and economic freedom in his *Capitalism and Freedom*. [25] He wrote that the great advances of civilization, whether in architecture or painting, in science or literature have never come from centralized government, as the latter can never duplicate the variety and diversity of individual creative expressions. Friedman maintained that economic freedom is necessarily linked to political freedom because both are expressions of one and the same impulse of individual autonomy against the coercive power of the state.

Both Hayek and Friedman were influenced by Popper who passionately defended democratic rule and freedom of thought:
It is the longing of uncounted unknown men to free themselves and their minds from the tutelage of authority and prejudice. It is their attempt to build up an open society which rejects the absolute authority of the merely established and the merely traditional, old or new, that measure up to their standards of freedom, of humaneness, and of rational criticism. [26]

24 Popper, K.R. (1966) *The Open Society and its Enemies*. Volume I. London: Routledge &Kegan Paul, p. 200
25 Friedman, M. (2002) *Capitalism and Freedom*; 40th anniversary edition. Chicago: Chicago University Press.
26 *The Open Society and its Enemies*, p. ix.

In short, *freedom and democracy* make possible the process of inventing new answers to the challenges of development. And freedom includes freedom of speech, the press, assembly, and religion.
The scholars mentioned above concluded that freedom and development *reinforce* one another; freedom of expression and freedom of the media facilitate the process of innovation in pursuit of economic development.

'...[a] country like Malaysia has enormous potential because we started at a very high level. In the 70s we competed with Singapore, Taiwan and South Korea. This was the level of Malaysia in the '70s. Now Singapore's GDP is five times as high as that of Malaysia, the GDP's of Taiwan,and South Korea are three times higher. I would then question why this is so. Is this because of the Islam we boast so much about? Or is it because of poor governance or poor accountability? No, it is because there are no free media to question the excesses, and due to the corruption endemic in the system'.. [27]

Transparency and the role of the media
Transparency plays a critical part in a country's economic development. Transparency isn't readily available; it has to be groomed. This grooming process is promoted by institutions in which individuals have the right of investigating and exposing relevant information to the public. It is the media in particular that serves this function; that is to say the autonomous version of the media, constituting the *Fourth Estate.*
The more resilient autonomous media can be, the better the chance that transparency exposes misdeeds or corrupt practices of individuals, enterprises and governments. Apart from having preventive effects, i.e., one will think twice before engaging in corruption, effective transparency prompts entrepreneurs and government to make better economic decisions and implement better public policies.
True, transparency is one element in a series of *checks and balances* that hold businesses and the body politic to account. This requires not only a functioning legal system that penalizes corruption and abuse of power, but also a free press that is essential to enable citizens to be properly informed about, e.g., violation of the law and shady deals.

27 Ibrahim, A. (2008) Democracy and Islam, by Anwar Ibrahim. In: *Democracy and Development*, p. 192.

Democracy and development

Easterly poses the question whether democracy is appropriate for very poor countries: Will a poor state – based on democratic principles – be able to promote economic growth? Conventional wisdom has it that democracy (including one of its cornerstones: freedom of expression) is at best irrelevant and at worst a hindrance to economic growth. *New York Times* columnist, Thomas Friedman, for example, wrote in one of his columns: *One-party non-democracy certainly has its drawbacks. But when it is led by a reasonably enlightened group of people, as China is today, it can also have great advantages. That one party can just impose the politically difficult but critically important policies needed to move a society forward in the 21ˢᵗ century.*

However, Daron Acemoglu et al. presented a paper in which they argue that democracy *does* promote growth. [28] Their main finding, based on extensive empirical analyses, is that democratization, i.e., the process of transition to democracy increases GDP per capita by about 20% in the long run.

It is in democracies that free media can inform citizens, who – equipped with this information – can hold government to account for its actions. Acemoglu et al. also demonstrate that democracy contributes to future economic development by increasing investment, encouraging economic reforms, improving the provision of public goods, like schooling and health care, and reducing social unrest. Hence, investing in economic growth *and* in health and education fosters economic development.

The factors: growth, health and education are precisely the component parts of the Human Development Index (HDI). [29] This index is, therefore, used in the analysis below to measure economic development.

Chapter I described the deterioration freedom of the press after the mid-1990s. This trend can also be observed in the democratisation process, which started in the mid-1970s with the end of the dictatorships in Portugal, Spain, and the military government of Greece. Samuel Huntington called it the *third wave* of democracy, characterized by the rule of law, an independent

28 Acemoglu, D., Naidu, S., Restrepo, P., Robinson, J. (1 May 2015) *Democracy Does Cause Growth*. To be downloaded via www.economist.com/democracy15
29 As regards education, Claus Moser, distinguished statistician and chairman of the British Royal Opera, once observed that education costs money, but then so does ignorance.

civil society, free and fair elections, and accountability. [30]

After the lost development decade of the 1980s, the democratisation idea was spreading across political movements in Latin America in the 1980s. Since the beginning of the 1990s the process shifted into higher gear in southern Africa (including the end of the apartheid regime in South Africa), as well as in the former Soviet Union after the fall of the Berlin Wall in 1989. Libertarian economists, such as Friedrich Hayek and Milton Friedman, saw their basic belief confirmed that market economies and democracy go together. A libertarian democracy is characterised by a free market and a small government, as enshrined in the *Washington Consensus*. It also included policy suggestions such as deregulation, privatisation of state enterprises and the protection of property rights.

As for Africa, the Washington Consensus recipe was applied in an attempt to put many near-bankrupt African countries back on their feet. However, an influential World Bank report identified that it was governance problems that posed obstacles to Africa's further development. Consequently, the donor community invested in the promotion of *good governance*, consisting of strengthening accountability, transparency, participation, and governments' responsiveness to the demands of the electorate – all important features of democracy. The idea was that democratisation would promote development and, in turn, development would further promote democratisation! The question then arose whether good governance in practice did indeed bring about development and the consolidation – if not further evolution – of democratic forms of government.

Thomas Carothers noted a gradual slowing down of the democratic trend since the beginning of this century; in many places the process even stagnated. Russia has moved backwards into a semi-authoritarian state. China is in a process of de-liberalisation, former Soviet countries are short on successful democracies, and in Latin America leaders such as the late Hugo Chavez in Venezuela, the Bolivian Evo Morales, Ecuadorian Rafael

---

30 The spread of different ideas about democracy go back to the middle of 1848; this was the first wave. The two World Wars were waged, at least on the part of the Allied Powers, in defence of democracy; this was the second wave, according to Huntington.

Correa (all involved in the *Bolivarian Revolution*), and Daniel Ortega of Nicaragua, call the shots. *Caudillismo*, i.e., the all powerful charismatic, near-authoritarian, leader appeared to be re-emerging in Latin America. [31]
Why this democracy backlash? One reason is that a good many fledgling democracies weren't able to 'deliver the goods', i.e., the population did not experience a general improvement in their material conditions. In other words, democracy is no guarantee for economic development. Carothers observed:

[a] return in some places to the notion that development requires a strong, i.e., non-democratic hand, which puts off democratisation until some indefinite future, and focuses on economic development and perhaps a little rule-of-law development. [32]

Another factor is China's growing international political and economic clout, in particular in Sub-Saharan Africa and Latin America. China is not likely to promote democracy in the countries with which it maintains political and economic relations. China appears less concerned about ethical and human rights issues in dealing with its overseas partners, nor is the country hindered by critical voices at home. All this is supported by China's investment in the media. In Africa, for instance, Howard French reports in *China's Second Continent* [33] that China's state broadcaster, CCTV, is building a continent-wide television power house in Nairobi, Kenya. The *China Daily* newspaper has launched a supplement entitled *African Weekly* for wide distribution throughout Africa. *Confucius Institutes* open their doors in more and more African countries.

    Carothers mentions a third factor, to wit America's loss of credibility

---

31 Developments into the direction of authoritarianism – and even totalitarianism – would be a recipe for censorship. Popper wrote in *The Open Society and its Enemies*, Vol. I: 'Totalitarianism, of course, cannot consider any criticism as friendly, since every criticism of such an authority must challenge the principle of authority itself', p. 189. Popper's central theme is the defence of the values of an open society, as opposed to a closed (tribal) society. By the sixth century B.C. democratic principles emerged in Athens among others promoted by trade and seafaring (read: economic development, PdH). One such value was, as Popper called it, 'that great spiritual revolution, the invention of critical discussion', p. 176.
32 Carothers, T. (2008) Does Democracy Promotion Have a Future? In: *Democracy and Development*. Amsterdam: KIT Publishers, 130.
33 French, H. W. (2014) *China's Second Continent*. New York: Knopf.

since its War on Terror. In short, there is scepticism about the benefits of democracy. All told, democracy cannot be forced upon a society; outsiders can be helpful but the decisive factor is the democratic aspirations of the society itself.

A fourth factor undermining democratic rule is the emergence of the growing number of strong rebel groups inspired by extremist religious beliefs. Some have been mentioned already, such as Boko Haram, and the Islamic State; others haven't as yet, but they belong to the same destabilising force undermining the authority of nation-states. The Lord's Resistance Army in Uganda, al-Qaeda in the Islamic Maghreb, and the Moro National Liberation Front in the Philippines, constitute just a few examples of a long list. Another development is the increasing popularity of populist and xenophobic political movements in Europe and America. The British magazine The Economist had this to say about it:

This newspaper stands for pretty much everything the populists despise: open markets, open borders, globalisation and the free movement of people. We do not expect to convince populist leaders of our arguments. But voters are reasonable – and most of them would sooner hear something more optimistic than rage against a dangerous world. Part of the answer is to draw on the power of liberal ideals. New technology, prosperity and commerce will do more than xenophobia to banish people's insecurities. The way to overcome resentment is economic growth- not to put up walls. [34]

The role of writers and culture in development
In economic terms poems, essays, and other works of art generate positive externalities (as economists would say), meaning that they inspire and widen the reader's horizon. Works of art set free 'the critical powers of man', as Karl Popper wrote, [35] and deepen the understanding of human behaviour. Writers' free flow of creativity, as expressed in their work, does benefit a society through its contribution to innovation, as Easterly emphasized, and thus to economic development.

---

34 The Economist, December 12 – 18, 2015, p.13.
35 The Open Society and its Enemies. Vol. I, p. 1.

George Orwell wrote in one of his columns that philosophers, writers, artists, even scientists, not only need encouragement and an audience, they need constant stimulation from other people. He concluded that when freedom of speech is taken away, the creative faculties dry up.

Welfare economics is closely associated with issues in the realm of consumers' preferences, including the consumption of cultural goods. Pieter Hennipman (1911-1994), professor emeritus of Amsterdam, was a pioneer in welfare economics.

He rejected the notion of the monstrosity (as he called it) of the *homo economicus*, the economically rational acting human being; humans don't act in an economically rational manner. There is no such thing as a specific economic purpose. Instead, Hennipman uses the term 'economic motive'. Any purpose, or goal, whose attainment requires the use of scarce resources can be considered an economic purpose, whether it be striving for maximum profit, or the publication of a collection of poems. Economic science has no authority, nor the instruments, to establish whether such a purpose makes sense or not.

Hennipman's definition of the *core function of economics* is the study of the most efficient provision of scarce resources for the satisfaction of individual preferences in order of their importance. This, Hennipman calls the 'economic principle'. [36]

Sufficient competition, which prevents the emergence of cartels, oligopolies, and monopolies, is an essential factor in explaining the results of an economy's functioning. Competition works well in a transparent environment. Transparency acts as a deterrent to corruption. As censorship can be used -and often is being used – to cover up corruption, one can conclude that the effective fight against corruption forms an integral part of Hennipman's economic principle.

---

36 Hennipman's terms: economic motive and economic principle derive from the extended version of his erudite doctoral thesis *Economisch Motief en Economisch Principe*; published by the Noord-Hollandse Uigevers Maatschappij in 1945. The thesis does not contain any mathematics. It is lucidly written. Some characterize Hennipman as a literary economist; which may have been due to his life companion, the South African poetess Elisabeth Eybers.

Tibor Scitovsky (1910-2002) wrote *The Joyless Economy* (1976). [37] This book analyses the behaviour of consumers of affluent societies who spend their money unwisely; they buy comfort at the detriment of joy in life. Scitovsky summarised what physiological psychologists had to say about human behaviour. The original way in which he treated the subject made him into a behavioural economist *avant la lettre*.

A central theme in *The Joyless Economy* is that puritan tradition, work ethic, and the educational system all contribute to depriving people of many of the skills and tastes necessary for the enjoyment of stimulating and creative leisure activities. The book challenges economists' unquestionable acceptance of the consumers' judgment of what is best for him, his tastes, and of his market behaviour as a reflection of his tastes. Scitovsky points out that it doesn't correspond with what psychologists have discovered about human's economic behaviour. His book offers, in his own words:

The groundwork for something humbler and better. The scientific approach, to my mind, is to observe bahavior- different people's behavior in similar situations and the same people's behavior in different situations – in order to find, contained in those observations, the regularities, the common elements, the seeming contradictions which then become the foundations of a theory to explain behavior. [38]

The Joyless Economy integrates elements of the insights of psychologists and economists into a more general theory of man's striving for satisfaction, and projecting it on the American way of life. After all, the most important motive force of behaviour, including consumption behaviour, is man's yearning for novelty, his desire to know the unknown. In Scitovsky's own words:

The yearning for new things and ideas is the source of all progress, all civilization; to ignore it as a source of satisfaction is surely wrong. [39]

---

37 Scitovsky, T. (1992) *The Joyless Economy; the Psychology of Human Satisfaction*. New York: Oxford University Press.
38 *The Joyless Economy*, xii-xiii.
39 Ibid., 11.

Dutch economist Rick van der Ploeg argues in his article In Art We Trust, that culture is an experience good; i.e., the more one 'consumes' culture, the more one gets out of it.[40] So, any additional 'consumption' of culture – reading a book, enjoying a play – carries an increasing marginal utility. Cultural goods are in fact investments in one's own cultural capital. Cultural goods should thus be viewed as social investment, contributing to the development of a society. Hence, censoring expressions of culture such as books, poems, plays, exhibitions, what have you, limits the development of a society, including its economic development. After all, a play, a concert, broadens the mind and the understanding of complex issues; a thought-provoking essay may offer fresh insights into, e.g., contemporary political issues.

Economics revolves around utility. Economic capital denotes the capacity to generate income or economic values, including knowledge. And economic value can be a means to generate social and cultural capital. The 'good life' must amount to more than the pursuit of economic wealth; it includes enjoying art and nature, a good conversation, the enjoyment of friendships.

The hypotheses tested
At the beginning of this chapter the question was posed whether there would be a relationship between censorship and economic growth and between censorship and economic development? To be able to answer the question, two hypotheses have been tested:

1 There is no relationship between the extent of censorship in a particular country and its economic growth trajectory; i.e., a country applying heavy censorship can still register economic growth.

2 There is a negative relationship between the extent of censorship and the level of economic development; i.e., the more stringent the censorship, the lower the economic development score.

---

40 Van der Ploeg, R. In Art We Trust. In: *De Economist*, Vol. 150, No.4, Oct. 2002, pp. 333 – 362.

In testing these two hypotheses, two criteria have been chosen. The first criterion is the annual economic growth percentage to indicate whether a country's economy is stagnant, grows modestly, or registers robust growth. Secondly, an acceptable measure of economic development is a country's position on the HDI list. [41] The HDI scores run from 1 (the highest score) to 0 (the lowest), so the HDI list starts with the best performing countries and ends with the poorest performers.

A regression analysis of the relationship between censorship and economic growth, plus censorship and economic development of a sample of 181 countries during the period 1980-2010 was undertaken. However, before presenting the results of the sample of 181 countries, a brief analysis of the most censored countries is presented.

The ten most censored countries

The CPJ published lists of the ten most censored countries in 2006, 2012, and 2015. [42] The 2006 and the 2015 list are presented below. The higher a country's position on that list, the stricter the censorship. A low HDI score means that the country scores badly in HDI terms.

For each censorship country its economic growth and HDI scores are entered.

---

41 HDI criteria are: life expectancy at birth, adult literacy rate, combined gross enrolment rate for primary, secondary, and tertiary education, and gross national income per capita.
42 CPJ staff judged countries according to 17 benchmarks. CPJ established the criteria after consultation with experts in the fields of press freedom, human rights, and media law. In order to appear on the list, countries had to meet at least 9 of the 17 criteria. The benchmarks included: abuse of independent media; existence of formal censorship regulations; state control of all media; state-sponsored violence against journalists; jamming of foreign news broadcasts; restrictions on Internet access; limits on journalists' mobility; interference in the production and distribution of publications; and existence of laws forbidding criticism.

Table 2: CPJ's 2006 most censored countries list and economic indicators

2006	% Ec. Growth*	HDI**
1. N. Korea	-	-
2. Myanmar	-	0.584
3. Turkmenistan	11.0	0.739
4. Eq. Guinea	-4.8	0.712
5. Libya	6.5	0.842
6. Eritrea	-1.0	0.467
7. Cuba	12.1	0.856
8. Uzbekistan	7.3	0.706
9. Syria	5.0	0.738
10.Belarus	10.0	0.819

* Source: World Development Indicators

** Source: 2006 HDI list.

Quite a few countries appear in CPJ's 2006 as well as in its 2015 list.

Table 3: CPJ's 2015 most censored countries list and economic indicators

2006	% Ec. Growth*	HDI**
1. Eritrea	1.7	0.381
2. N.Korea	-	-
3. Saudi Arabia	3.5	0.836
4. Ethiopia	9.9	0.435
5. Azerbaijan	2.0	0.747
6. Vietnam	6.0	0.638
7. Iran	1.5	0.749
8. China	7.4	0.719
9. Myanmar	8.5	0.524
10.Cuba	2.7 (2013	0.815

* Source: World Development Indicators

** Source: 2014 HDI list.

One of the newcomers on the 2015 list is China, taking up position 8. A prominent reason why China is included in the list is because of the way it goes about censorship, as described in the box below.

Each year, the General Administration of Press and Publication (GAPP) – the government body responsible for censoring publications – releases a list to each news agency that contains a list of blacklisted keywords. The GAPP releases at least thirty of these lists on a yearly basis, frequently changing the content of the list in order to accurately reflect the ever-changing political situation. Some sensitive keywords – such as 'Tiananmen Square' – remain on the list indefinitely. Some blacklisted keywords may cover a wide range of topics, whereas the descriptions of other keywords are vague sometimes. This makes it hard to define a clear boundary on what is acceptable – and what not; thus making the censorship system even harder to understand than it already is'. From: *Drugs for the Mind*, by Sofie Sun. Amsterdam: Eva Tas Foundation (2015)

Some observations

From the two CPJ lists, a group of most notorious countries during the past decade can be deduced from the ones that appear on both lists: Myanmar, Cuba, Eritrea, and North Korea. Of these, Eritrea and North Korea are the worst of the worst countries, while Myanmar and Cuba have improved over time: Cuba dropped from 7th (2006) to 10th position (2015) on the list (remember: the lower on the list, the less censorship) while Myanmar dropped even more dramatically from 2nd (2006) to 9th position (2015). The question is whether Myanmar's and Cuba's lowering censorship scores in the period 2006-2015 translated in better economic development performance. While Cuba's economic growth went down from 2006 to 2014, the country climbed from 51st to 44th place on the HDI list. Myanmar, however, didn't change its HDI ranking: 150 in both 2006 and 2014, although the number of countries on the HDI list increased in 2014.

Myanmar's drop on the list was mainly due to its discontinuance in 2012 of the more than four decades of pre-publication censorship. But its media remains tightly controlled: Myanmar's *Printers and Publishers Registration Law*, enacted in March 2014, bans news that could be considered insulting to religion, disturbing to the rule of law, or harmful to ethnic unity.

Cuba's improved status is the result of the elimination of exit visas that prohibited most foreign travel for its citizens for decades. Yet, Cuba continues to have the most restricted climate of press freedom in the Americas. The internet has opened up some space for critical reporting, but service providers are ordered to block objectionable content.

As regards Eritrea, its HDI ranking worsened from 157th place in 2006 to 182nd place in 2014; this is in line with its rise in the CPJ list from position 6 to heading the list in 2015.

Now, if one were to take most countries included in the 2006 and 2015 CPJ lists, the conclusion is that – by and large – they didn't score well in economic development (read: HDI ranking) terms.[43] Only two censorship countries belong to the 'high development' and 'very high development' HDI groups: Cuba and Saudi Arabia – an odd couple, so to speak. Cuba's high HDI position is explained by its relatively good health and education performance, while Saudi Arabia's high score is thanks to being the world's largest oil producer, which pushed up its GDP per capita up.

The observations above seem to confirm the second hypothesis: the more censorship a country exerts, the lower its HDI score. As to hypothesis one: countries that apply strong censorship can register robust annual economic growth. This hypothesis seems to have been confirmed as well, as high-censorship countries in both tables, such as Ethiopia and Turkmenistan, boasted robust growth, while low-ranking countries, such as Belarus, and Myanmar also registered high growth percentages.

Broader sample
Obviously, the CPJ list sample is too small. Therefore, a broader sample was taken from the *Global Press Freedom* index prepared by FH since 1980. Four years were chosen: 1980, 1990, 2000, and 2010, analysing 181 countries for at least one of these periods. Each country is categorised on the basis of its press freedom: Free (1), Partly Free (2), and Not Free (3). The selection criteria applied by FH are included in Annexe I.

---

43 The HDI index identifies the following country groups: as regards the 2005 HDI: low development index (156 -177); medium development index (71 – 155); high development index (1 – 70). The 2015 HDI list ranks the following country groups: low development index (145 – 187); medium development index (103 – 144), high development index (50 – 102), and very high development index (1 – 49).

The HDI index variable is taken from the United Nations Development Program (UNDP) reports concerned. The economic growth variable is taken from the World Bank's *World Development Indicators*.

Linear panel data regressions were run to test the relationship between the level of press freedom and the HDI index. In addition, press freedom's relationship with economic growth was also tested. No control variables were applied, such as macroeconomic variables or the quality of institutions. The results are reflected in the *dot plot* presentations in Annexe II.

The first finding is that countries that have a Free status (1) typically score higher on the HDI index compared to the Partly Free (2) and Not Free (3) countries. The line in the graph concerned is the regression line that fits best for these values; it shows a downward slope.

The results of the panel regressions on the effects of press freedom on economic growth show a different picture. There is a slightly upward regression line, indicating that there is hardly any relationship between the two. Free countries don't register higher economic growth percentages than Partly Free and Not Free countries. In fact, Partly Free and Not Free countries even register slightly higher economic growth rates. One should be careful, however, in drawing conclusions, as the low R-squared for this regression indicates a low fit for the model.

The press freedom-economic growth dot plot shows a few *outliers* with economic growth exceeding plus 15% or minus 15%. Excluding these countries in the analysis results in broadly the same outcome as the one which included them.

Reverse relationship
When doing regression analyses, reverse relationships are analysed as well to confirm that there would indeed be a relationship between two (or more) phenomena at hand. Should the reverse analysis not demonstrate a relationship as established in the original regression analysis, it means that other factors also impinge upon the relationship.

The results of the reverse regression analyses are reflected below.

They confirm that there is indeed a relationship between economic development and press freedom: the better the HDI score the freer the press is. An example: a 0.4 improvement in a country's HDI score would result in the country's promotion to a better press freedom category. Hence investing in better HDI reinforces press freedom.

The reverse regression analysis shows that there is a negative relationship between growth and press freedom; i.e., better economic growth would result in less press freedom. This outcome, however, should be taken with a big pinch of salt, in that a 10% increase in economic growth would result in only a 0.2 points worsening in a country's ranking regarding press freedom. So, the relationship is a rather weak one.

The reverse regression exercise was also done excluding the outliers as mentioned above; however, the result was that without the outliers the outcome would be the same, as the differences were insignificant.

Conclusions

The main conclusion is that both hypotheses are confirmed by the outcomes of the sample.

Regarding the first hypothesis, the sample shows that there is no clear relationship between the level of press freedom and the percentage of economic growth. Although our sample suggests that countries with bad press freedom scores do slightly better in economic growth terms; given the low R-squared for this regression, this outcome must be treated with caution.

As for the second hypothesis, our sample shows that lower press freedom does coincide with a lower HDI score: the better the HDI score the freer the press is. Investment in better HDI appears to improve press freedom.

Our finding regarding the relationship between press freedom and development is confirmed in the literature. For example, the UNESCO study *Press Freedom and Development* states the following:

While no conclusion can be reached as to the existence of causality between freedom of the press and the different variables explored, all the findings confirm the importance of press freedom for development. A free press always has a positive influence, whether it be on poverty and its different aspects (monetary poverty and access to primary commodities, health and education), on governance or on violence and conflict issues.....it holds governments accountable and makes their actions more transparent. [44]

Although the UNESCO report applies a broad definition of development, it coincides to a large extent with the composite parts of HDI, as applied in our sample in measuring economic development.

Our finding on the lack of a relationship between press freedom and economic growth is, however, not confirmed across the board, despite the fact that quite a few authoritarian regimes, applying strict censorship, register high economic growth percentages. [45] There is ample room for further research in this realm, distinguishing clearly between the terms 'economic growth' and 'economic development', and introducing control variables, as noted above.

It would also be interesting to investigate what the possible tipping points might be. The question here is what the factors are that would help transform economic growth into economic development. And – given the subject of this essay – what possible role the free media could play in this transformation process.

---

44 UNESCO (2008) *Press Freedom and Development*, p.5.
45 Alam, A., Shah, S.Z. (2013) *The Role of Press Freedom in Economic development: A Global Perspective*; In: Journal of Media Economics, Vol. 26, Issue 1, 2013. The authors maintain that there is a bidirectional relationship between press freedom and economic growth.

CHAPTER III

DEFENDERS OF FREEDOM OF EXPRESSION AND FREEDOM OF THE MEDIA

The typical censorship environment is created by authoritarian regimes and extremist organisations that don't care what others say about their actions. They are in full control of the media, censor all information, block internet access, and molest, persecute and even kill dissenters. That is the environment that brave individuals and international organisations encounter when they try to do something about it.

That 'something' consists often of protecting, assisting, and defending the rights of journalists, writers, and bloggers – the prime victims of censorship. Another form of support is to bring censorship to the attention of appropriate institutions that – in turn – can exert pressure on the censors to abide by Article 19 of the Universal Declaration of Human Rights (UDHR) and related international covenants they have signed on to. The challenge faced by defenders of the freedom of expression is a daunting one; however, looking away is not an option because that will only perpetuate or even worsen censorship.

Which are the organisations that don't look away; what is their mission, and what have they been able to achieve? This chapter provides an overview of the most prominent ones involved in defending freedom of expression and freedom of the media.

_ Committee to Protect Journalists
'When journalists can't speak, we speak up'. This is the motto of the Committee to Protect Journalists (CPJ), founded in 1981 by a group of U.S. correspondents who realized they could not ignore the plight of colleagues whose reporting put them in peril.

The idea that journalists around the world should come together to defend the rights of colleagues working in repressive and dangerous environments led to CPJ's first advocacy campaign in 1982. At the time, three British journalists were arrested in Argentina while covering the Falklands War. A letter from CPJ Honorary Chairman Walter Cronkite helped release them from prison. Since then, CPJ's mission involves not only journalists but anyone who cherishes the value of information for a free society.

CPJ promotes press freedom worldwide and defends the right of journalists to report the news without fear of reprisal. CPJ defends the free flow of news and commentary by taking action wherever journalists are attacked, imprisoned, killed, kidnapped, threatened, censored, or harassed. Journalism plays a vital role in the balance of power between a government and its people. When a country's journalists are silenced, its people are silenced. By protecting journalists, CPJ protects freedom of expression and democracy.

CPJ publishes annually a list of 10 *Most Censored Countries* as part of CPJ's annual publications. CPJ's Press Freedom Award 2015 went to the Syrian weblog *Raqqa is Being Slaughtered*, for its reporting on IS atrocities.

Support programs
When necessary, CPJ lobbies governments or international agencies to help secure refugee or asylum status for journalists. CPJ also provides logistical support to journalists when they resettle in exile. In addition, it refers journalists to financial resources, including information on grants, fellowships, and awards. CPJ steps in when journalists are persecuted for their reporting and find themselves in dire situations. Some examples of CPJ's work include:
- Helping get medical care for journalists following brutal assaults or for journalists suffering from mistreatment in prison.
- Supporting journalists forced to go into hiding or to relocate within their countries to escape threats from local officials, militia, or criminal gangs.
- Contributing to legal funds for journalists facing prison sentences. •
- Evacuating journalists at risk into temporary havens.
- Providing support for families of imprisoned journalists.

CPJ provides financial support and modest grants to journalists at risk through its *Gene Roberts Emergency Fund*. To apply for an emergency grant, journalists must complete and submit a request form, which will be reviewed by CPJ staff.

Contact
Committee to Protect Journalists
330 7th Avenue, 11th Floor
New York, NY 10001
Tel +1 212-465-1004
info@cpj.org

_ Reporters without Borders

Reporters Without Borders (RWB), or *Reporters Sans Frontières* (RSF), is a France-based international non-governmental organisation that promotes and defends freedom of information and freedom of the press. RWB has consultant status at the United Nations.

RWB has two primary spheres of activity: one is focused on internet censorship and the new media, and the other on providing material, financial and psychological assistance to journalists assigned to dangerous areas.

RWB's objectives are to: (i) monitor attacks on freedom of information worldwide; (ii) denounce any such attacks in the media; (iii) act in cooperation with governments to fight censorship and laws aimed at restricting freedom of information; (iv) financially assist persecuted journalists, as well as their families; and, (v) offer material assistance to war correspondents in order to enhance their safety.

RWB was founded in 1985, in Montpellier, France. Its head office is in Paris. RWB also maintains offices in Berlin, Brussels, Geneva, Madrid, Rome, Stockholm, Tunis, Vienna, and Washington D.C.

RWB draws its inspiration from Article 19 of the UDHR, according to which everyone has "the right to freedom of opinion and expression" and also the right to "seek, receive and impart" information and ideas "regardless of frontiers."

RWB's means of direct action are appeals to government authorities through letters or petitions, as well as through frequent press releases. Through its world-wide network of roughly 150 correspondents, RWB gathers information and conducts investigations of press freedom violations by geographical region or topic. If necessary, it will send a team of its own to assess working conditions for journalists in a specific country.

RWB releases annual reports on countries as well as its *Press Freedom Index*. It has launched advertising campaigns with the assistance of advertising firms to raise public awareness of threats to freedom of information and freedom of the press, to undermine the image of countries that it considers enemies of freedom of expression, and to discourage political support for governments that attack rather than protect freedom of information. The campaigns are circulated to the media, international organisations, government agencies, and educational institutions using the internet as well as traditional media channels.

RWB also provides financial assistance to journalists and media that are either in danger or are having difficulty surviving, through providing funds to assist exiled or imprisoned journalists and their families, and to families of journalists who have been killed. Financial assistance is also given to journalists who have to leave their home countries; to repair the effects of vandalism on media outlets; to cover the legal fees of journalists who have been persecuted for their writings or the medical bills of those who have been physically attacked; and to provide bullet-proof vests for use by journalists.

Each December RWB publishes an annual overview of events related to freedom of information and the safety of journalists. It maintains a website (www.rsf.org) accessible in six languages.

Starting in 2001, RWB has published its annual *Predators of Press Freedom* list which highlights what it feels are the worst violators of press freedom.

RWB maintains a *Press Freedom Barometer* on its website showing the number of journalists, media assistants, netizens, and citizen journalists killed or imprisoned during a year. In conjunction with its World Day against Cyber Censorship, RWB updates its *Enemies of the Internet* and *Countries under Surveillance* lists. Regarding *Enemies of the Internet*, RWB classifies a country as an enemy of the internet because "all of these countries mark themselves out not just for their capacity to censor news and information online but also for their almost systematic repression of Internet users."

RWB launched the first *International Online Free Expression Day* on 12 March 2008. Now named *World Day against Cyber Censorship*, this annual event rallies support for an unrestricted internet, accessible to all. On the same date RWB awards its *Netizen Prize* and issues its report on freedom of information in cyberspace and its *Enemies of the Internet* list.

Contact
Reporters Without Borders/ Reporters Sans Frontières
CS 90247
75083 Paris Cedex 02
France
Phone: +33 1 44 83 84 84
Email: assistance@rsf.org

_ Article 19

ARTICLE 19 pictures a world where people are free to speak their opinion, to participate in decision-making and to make informed choices about their lives. To make this possible, people everywhere must be able to exercise their rights to freedom of expression and freedom of information. Without these rights, democracy, good governance, and economic development cannot happen.

ARTICLE 19 was founded in 1987. It is registered and regulated in the UK, Bangladesh, Brazil, Kenya, Mexico, Senegal, Tunisia, and the USA. American businessman and philanthropist J. Roderick MacArthur originally imagined the establishment of an organisation that would defend the right to freedom of expression. After MacArthur's death in 1984, Martin Ennals, a former director of Amnesty International, was asked to develop a proposal for a new organistion to be called ARTICLE 19.

ARTICLE 19 has worked and partnered with International Organisations like the United Nations, with Non-Governmental Organisations such as Amnesty International and International Media Support, and with governments such as the UK and Brazil.

ARTICLE 19's first campaign was on behalf of Zwelakhe Sisulu, a South African editor who was detained without trial by the South African apartheid government one month after he was elected as a member of ARTICLE 19's International Board. Sisulu was released in 1988 following the campaign.

In 1988, ARTICLE 19's second campaign, mounted in cooperation with CPJ, focused on publishing of the report 'Journalism under Occupation: Israel's Regulation of the Palestinian Press'.
A year later, the Iranian leader Ayatollah Khomeini issued a fatwa against the author Salman Rushdie and his publishers for alleged blasphemy in his novel 'The Satanic Verses'. ARTICLE 19 partnered with American PEN to lead a campaign for the protection of Salman Rushdie, called the International Rushdie Defence Campaign. On 25 September 1998, Salman Rushdie officially came out of hiding at an ARTICLE 19 press conference after the Iranian government formally lifted the fatwa against him.

For the last 10 years, ARTICLE 19 has organised the 'four tenors' meetings, bringing together the UN, the Organization of American States, the African Union, and the Organization for Security and Cooperation in Europe 'special procedures', the general name given to the mechanisms established by the UN Human Rights Council and other inter-governmental institutions to address either specific country situations or thematic issues in all parts of the world. Special Rapporteurs on freedom of expression and freedom of the media formulate joint statements on key topical and sensitive issues.

Article 19 is a founding member of the *International Freedom of Expression Exchange* (IFEX), a clearing house for a global network of NGOs that monitor free expression violations worldwide. It is also a member of the *Tunesia Monitoring Group* of 21 free expression organisations that lobbied the Tunesian government to improve its human rights record. And it is the coordinator of the *International Partnership Group for Azerbaijan* (IPGA), a coalition to promote and protect freedom of expression in Azerbaijan. Article 19 is a founding member of the *Freedom of Information Advocates* (FOIA) Network, a global forum that aims to support campaigning, advocacy, and fundraising on access to information through the exchange of information, ideas and strategies. The FOIA Network also aims to facilitate the formation of regional or international coalitions to address access to information issues.

Contact
ARTICLE 19 Headquarters
Free Word Centre
60 Farringdon Road
London EC1R 3GA
United Kingdom
Tel: +44 20 7324 2500
Email: info@article19.org

_ The Rory Pack Trust

The Rory Pack Trust was established in 1995 in memory of freelance cameraman Rory Peck who was killed in Moscow in 1993. The Trust is totally independent and relies on contributions from corporations, trusts, foundations, and individuals to carry out its work.

The principal objectives of the Trust are (i) to provide practical assistance and support to freelance news gatherers and their families worldwide, (ii) to raise their profile, promote their welfare and safety, and (iii) to support their right to report freely and without fear. One recent example of practical assistance is the *Syria Media Safety Resource*, an information tool that Syrian reporters need to help them work more safely and to streamline their access to emergency assistance. This tool was developed together with CPJ and a coalition of international organisations of journalists.

The Trust believes that freelancers play an important and integral role within newsgathering and see the Trust's role in protecting and supporting them as a practical and significant contribution to independent journalism and the free flow of information. Based in London, the Trust works globally with a network of international and local partners.

The Trust runs a freelance assistance program. There is also the Rory Pack Award. The *Freelance Assistance Program* is at the heart of the Trust's work, providing financial and practical support to freelance journalists and their families globally. Its partnerships enable the Trust to reach freelancers in countries where it is difficult to operate and to provide additional support where needed. The Program operates in four main areas:

Assistance grants provide financial assistance to freelance news gatherers in crisis, and to those who have been seriously injured or are suffering persecution, exile or imprisonment as a result of their work. They also support the families of those who have lost their lives. The website contains information about freelancers assisted through this program. *Rory Pack Training Bursaries* make hostile environment training affordable for freelancers, enabling them to gain the skills and knowledge needed to work in difficult and dangerous environments.

Region specific projects, run in collaboration with local and international partners, protect and educate freelancers in practical ways that are specific to their needs.

Ongoing practical advice and information for freelancers and their families is a unique and essential source of guidance, support and referral. Regarding the Rory Pack Awards, there are three of them: (i) the Rory Pack Award for News, (ii) the Rory Pack Award for News Features, and (iii) the Sony Impact Award for Current Affairs. The Rory Peck Awards welcomes self-funded entries from local freelancers, especially those living and working in regions where it is difficult to operate.

Contact
The Rory Peck Trust
Linton House
24 Wells Street
London
W1T 3PH
United Kingdom
Tel: +44 (0)203 219 7860
info@rorypecktrust.org

_ The International Federation of Journalists

The International Federation of Journalists (IFJ) is the world's largest
organisation of journalists. It was first established in 1926; it has been in its
present form since 1952. Today the Federation represents around 600,000
members in 134 countries.

The IFJ promotes international action to defend press freedom
and social justice through strong, free, and independent trade unions of
journalists. The IFJ does not subscribe to any given political viewpoint, but
promotes human rights, democracy, and pluralism. The IFJ is opposed to
discrimination of all kinds and condemns the use of media as propaganda or
to promote intolerance and conflict.

The IFJ believes in freedom of political and cultural expression
and defends trade unions and other basic human rights. The IFJ is the
organisation that speaks for journalists within the UN system and within the
international trade union movement.

The IFJ supports journalists and their unions whenever they are
fighting for their industrial and professional rights and has established an
International Safety Fund to provide humanitarian aid for journalists in need.
The growing trend among media organisations to use right-grabbing
contracts has become a matter of great concern for the International and the

European Federation of Journalists (IFJ/EFJ). As a result, the IFJ and the EFJ have launched a European-wide campaign against right-grabbing contracts and demand fair payments to journalists.

The IFJ issues *The International Press Card*; an instantly and internationally recognizable professional identification. The International Press Card (IPC) is recognised the world over and is the only press pass endorsed by national journalists' groups in more than 130 countries. It provides instant confirmation that the bearer is a working journalist. It is only issued to journalists who are committed to ethical standards and solidarity between media professionals.

The card represents an acknowledgment of journalists' commitment to ethical standards and IFJ's Code of Ethics. IPC card holders belong to the IFJ family. The IPC connects journalists globally and ensures that IFJ affiliated organisations extend to the IPC bearer assistance and courtesy in the performance of her/his mission.

Journalists travelling in conflict zones have testified to the benefits of the IPC. It has helped many journalists get out of tricky situations in dealing with soldiers, police, or officials. The IPC facilitates access to official meetings. Holders can take advantage of the IFJs official recognition within the European Union (EU) and within the agencies of the UN. Not least, the IPC will help journalists in many countries gain privileged access to media events – this is never guaranteed, but the card gives journalists a better chance of success than any other international accreditation.

The IFJ provides support and services to press card holders, including access to the IFEX network which is a coalition of press freedom and journalists' groups that monitors the state of press freedom the world over. Regular bulletins from the IFJ and updates on actions in defence of journalists are available to all card holders.

Contact
IPC-Residence Palace, Bloc C
Rue de la Loi 155
B-1040 Brussels

Belgium
Telephone: +32 (0)2 235 22 00
E-Mail: ifj(at)ifj .org

_ Journalists in Distress Fund
The Canadian Journalists For Free Expression's *Journalists in Distress Fund*
provides humanitarian assistance to journalists whose lives and well-being
are threatened because of their profession.
Essential information about the Journalists in Distress Fund:
- The recipient must be a journalist, vetted or verified by either an IFEX
  member or an organisation that provides journalist assistance.
- Preference is given to cases where danger to the journalist is imminent
  or the situation is urgent.
- The amount granted typically ranges from $500 to $1500 CDN,
  depending on the case.
- Journalists are eligible for a maximum of two separate grants from CJFE.
  What support does the Journalists in Distress Fund provide?
- Lawyers' fees when journalists are detained.
- Medical expenses when they are caught in the line of fire or traumatised
  by their coverage.
- Transportation costs when they are forced to flee.
- Financial support for the families of journalists who have been killed
  or imprisoned.
- Resettlement costs within first year of arriving in final safe country.
To learn more about the Journalists in Distress Fund, or to request the
application form in Word instead of PDF format, contact **jid@cjfe.org**.

Contact
Canadian Journalists for Free Expression (CJFE)
555 Richmond St. W., Suite 1101, P.O. Box 407,
Toronto, ON
Canada

M5V 3B1
Phone: 416-515-9622
Email: cjfe@cjfe.org
Website: www.cjfe.org
Facebook: canadaCJFE
Twitter: @canadaCJFE

_ Index on Censorship

Index on Censorship is a campaigning and publishing organisation for freedom of expression, which produces a quarterly magazine of the same name. It is directed by the non-profit *Writers and Scholars International, Ltd.* (WSI) in association with *Index on Censorship*.

The original inspiration for Index on Censorship came from two prominent Soviet dissidents, Pavel Litvinov, and Larisa Bogoraz, the former wife of the writer, Yuli Daniel, who had written to *The Times* in 1968 calling for international condemnation of the rigged trial of two young writers and their typists on charges of 'anti-Soviet agitation and propaganda'.

Stephen Spender, the British poet, novelist, and essayist, organised a telegram of support and sympathy from 16 British and US intellectuals, including W. H. Auden, Yehudi Menuhin, Henry Moore, Bertrand Russell, and Igor Stravinsky. Litvinov then suggested, in a letter later published in Index's first issue, the need for some sort of publication "to provide information to world public opinion about the real state of affairs in the USSR".

Spender and his colleagues sought to go further than this, wishing to cover then current censorship in right-wing dictatorships such as Greece, Spain, Portugal, and the military regimes of Latin America, as well as in the former Soviet Union and its satellites.

Index on Censorship runs a program of UK-based and international projects that put the organisation's philosophy into practice. In 2009 and 2010 Index on Censorship worked in Afghanistan, Burma, Iraq, Tunisia and many other countries, in support of journalists, broadcasters, artists, and writers who work against a backdrop of intimidation, repression, and censorship.

Index on Censorship magazine supports free expression, publishing distinguished writers from around the world, exposing suppressed stories, initiating debate, and providing an international record of censorship. The quarterly editions of the magazine usually focus on a country, region, or a recurring theme in the global free expression debate.

The magazine has sought to shed light on other challenges facing free expression, including religious extremism, the rise of nationalism, and internet censorship. Issues are usually organised by theme, and contain a country-by-country list of recent cases involving censorship, restrictions on freedom of the press, and other free speech violations.

Occasionally, *Index on Censorship* publishes short works of fiction and poetry by notable new writers as well as censored ones. The Russia issue (January 2008) won the *Amnesty International Media Award* 2008. In addition to print and annual subscriptions, *Index on Censorship* is available as an application for the iPhone/iPad.

The Index on Censorship website http://www.indexoncensorship. org provides the hub for all its published writing, events and programs. It carries some content from *Index on Censorship* magazine, but mostly originally commissioned articles and blogs on free expression issues.

The site also has an extensive archive of resources that offers a searchable global listing of organisations and media that champion freedom of expression; reports surveying freedom of expression around the world; links to censorship circumvention guides and software; and internet censorship. The archive also holds a selection of the best writing about landmark issues in the fight for free expression over the years, such as the controversy surrounding the publication of *Jyllands Posten's* Muhammad cartoons in Denmark, and internet censorship. It provides information about all current events, issues of magazines and projects that Index is undertaking.

Index's *arts programs* investigate the impact of current and recent social and political change on arts practitioners, assessing the degree and depth of self-censorship. Index on Censorship commissions internationally new work, including new photography, film & video, visual arts and performances. Recent examples include an exhibition of photo stories produced by women in Iraq: *Open Shutters*; and a program involving artists from refugee and migrant communities in the UK, linking with artists from their country of origin. Index also commissioned a new play by *Actors for Human Rights: Seven Years With Hard Labour*, weaving together four accounts from former Burmese political prisoners now living in the UK. Index also co-published a book of poetry by homeless people in London and St. Petersburg.

Index on Censorship annually presents awards to courageous journalists, writers, artists, lawyers, innovators, campaigners, and whistleblowers from around the world who have made a significant contribution to free expression over the past year.

Contact
Index on Censorship
92-94 Tooley St,
London SE1 2TH,
United Kingdom
Phone:+44 20 7260 2660

_ Free Press Unlimited

Free Press Unlimited (FPL) is a foundation based in Amsterdam, the Netherlands. Its Executive Board is made up of Leon Willems and Ruth Kronenburg. Together they head a dedicated team of some 44 professionals. Its media projects in 36 countries around the world are overseen by Programme Coordinators, who specialise in particular fields and/or geographic areas.

FPL observes that we all need reliable news and relevant information, to know what's going on in our community, and in the world at large, to stay clear of danger, rid ourselves of harmful preconceptions, stand up for ourselves and take advantage of new opportunities. Honest reporting can open one's eyes, and expand one's horizon – particularly when living in an unstable or impoverished region.

Free Press Unlimited wants people to have access to the information they need to develop and prosper. People deserve to know.

Reporters Respond gives financial aid to journalists, producers, and cameramen and women who are at risk because of their profession. Reporters Respond provides help quickly. This fast, small scale, financial support can help prevent more serious damage and enables journalists, producers, and cameramen and women to continue to do their job.
To apply, download the application form at the bottom of this page. Email the completed form to reportersrespond@freepressunlimited.org.

Contact
Free Press Unlimited
Weesperstraat 3
1018 DN Amsterdam
The Netherlands
Email: info@freepressunlimited.org
Tel: +316 1306 7684.

_ Freedom House

FH is an independent watchdog organisation dedicated to the expansion of freedom around the world. Freedom House speaks out against the main threats to democracy and empowers citizens to exercise their fundamental rights. Founded in 1941, FH was the first American organisation to champion the advancement of freedom globally.

In 1973, FH launched what is now its flagship publication, *Freedom in the World*, an annual survey of global political rights and civil liberties. Employing a methodology devised by leading social scientists, the survey analyzes and rates every country in the world on a series of fundamental freedom indicators. Its results are always highly anticipated because it provides policymakers, journalists, and the public a comprehensive view of the global state of freedom.

The 1997 merger with the *National Forum Foundation* substantially enhanced Freedom House's capacity to conduct on-the-ground projects in fledgling democracies in Central and Eastern Europe, the Balkans, and the former Soviet Union. FH assisted these post-Communist societies in establishing independent media, independent think tanks, and the core institutions of electoral politics.

FH also publishes an annual *Global Press Freedom Report*. This publication presents trends in press freedom (or the lack thereof), provides thoroughly researched country analyses, and a list of 'Free', 'Partly Free', and 'Not Free' countries and territories. An updated list of *'Worst of the worst'* performing countries forms part of these annual reports.

FH sponsored conferences highlighting North Korea's human rights abuses in Washington, DC; Seoul, South Korea; Brussels, Belgium; and Rome, Italy.

The *New Generation of Advocate Fellows* program expands the horizons of young civil society leaders in the Middle East and North Africa by offering visiting fellowships with counterpart organisations in the U.S. FH and *Human Rights First* hosted a human rights summit bringing together human rights defenders from around the world to develop a Plan of Action to advance global human rights. They met with President Barack Obama, US policy makers, and influential figures from the world of media, think tanks, universities, NGOs and other activists to shed light on the human rights situation in their own countries.

Contact
Freedom House National Headquarters
1850 M Street NW, Suite 1100
Washington, District of Columbia   20036
United States
Phone: 202-296-5101
Fax: 202-293-2840
info@freedomhouse.org

_ PEN International

PEN International brings together writers, journalists, poets – all those using the written word to promote ideas in the common belief that it is through this sharing that bridges of understanding can be built between peoples. These bridges cross political, geographical, ethnic, cultural, religious and other divides.

The protection of the right of freedom of expression – the freedom to express ideas without fear of attack, arrest or other types of persecution – has been at the heart of PEN's work since it was founded in 1921 by Amy Dawson Scott and John Galsworthy.

PEN's Charter pledges that all members will oppose any form of suppression of freedom of expression in the country and community to which they belong, as well as throughout the world wherever possible. PEN International celebrates literature and promotes freedom of expression. PEN's global community of writers now comprises 144 PEN centers spanning more than 100 countries. PEN's programs, campaigns, events, and publications connect writers and readers to enhance global solidarity and cooperation. PEN International is a non-political organisation and holds consultative status at the UN and UNESCO.

Contact
PEN International,
Brownlow House,
50 – 51 High Holborn,
London WC1V 6ER
United Kingdom
+44 (0) 20 7405 0338
info@pen-international.org

_ Writers in Prison Committee

PEN International has various committees; including the *Writers in Prison Committee* (WiPC). This committee works on behalf of persecuted writers worldwide. It was established in 1960 in response to increasing attempts to silence voices of dissent by imprisoning writers and journalists.

WiPC monitors between 700-1,000 cases across the globe each year. The WiPC mobilises the wider PEN community to take action through its *Rapid Action Network* (RAN) alerts, targeted regional campaigns, and by utilizing PEN's consultative status with the UN to submit country reports. The WiPC also works through the UN to bring attention to individual cases and to systemic human rights problems in specific countries. The Committee also works closely with the International Cities Refugee Network (ICORN). The RAN alerts provide details of cases of individuals whose lives and liberty are being threatened and make specific suggestions for action.

In addition to its work on behalf of individual writers, the Committee launches campaigns on issues affecting freedom of expression, such as Religious Defamation, Impunity and Criminal Defamation, and campaigns focused on specific regions or countries, such as the Americas, Iran, China and Turkey.

Twice a year WiPC produces a *case list* of individuals around the world who are detained or otherwise persecuted for their peaceful political activities or for the practice of their profession.

The freedom of expression work of PEN, and specifically that of the WiPC team in London is evolving; it is no longer entirely focused on the *case list* with the sole intention of creating urgent calls to actions: the RANs. Increasingly the work of the WiPC team is the foundation of all of PEN's freedom of expression work, including analysis of cases and regional issues, research, campaigning, working together with other staff, thinking regionally, and long-term planning.

Contact
PEN International/ WiPC,
50-51 High Holborn
London WC1V6ER
United Kingdom

Phone: +44 (0) 20 7405 0338
Email: info@pen-international.org

_ PEN Emergency Fund
PEN also assists financially writers who have been detained through the
PEN Emergency Fund. This fund was established in 1971 by Dutch writer A.
Den Doolaard (then also vice-president of PEN International). The initial
beneficiaries of the Emergency Fund were writers in Eastern Europe. Once
the Berlin Wall had fallen, the Fund's emphasis shifted to African and Asian
countries. Now the Fund's main emphasis is on the Middle East and Iran.
The Fund receives donations mainly from the Dutch PEN membership and
from some other PEN-centres. In addition, there are a few Dutch donor
agencies supporting the Fund, such as the Lira Foundation which has a
special position in the secondary exploitation of the copyrights of authors
and translators in the Netherlands. The Democracy and Media Foundation
runs an endowment fund, investing in Dutch newspapers. A portion of the
proceeds is invested in the promotion of pluralism in the media landscape.
The foundation also supports initiatives and organisations, such as the
PEN Emergency Fund, that contribute to a strong, honest, and inclusive
democratic rule of law, as well as critical, independent media. At the
moment, the Foundation Prisoners of Conscience is the only foreign donor.
In the past OxfamNovib was one of the donors; but now only funds the
annual OxfamNovibPEN-awards.

The Emergency Fund's present funding base is very small; hence
future support to victims of censorship will be limited.

In its 2014 annual report the Emergency Fund wrote that the
Fund was able to provide support to writers in fourteen countries. The
largest contributions went to affected writers in Syria and Iran. Smaller
contributions went to writers in the Gulf States, Central America, Africa,
Asia, The Middle East, and Russia. Names of the beneficiaries were not
mentioned to protect their own safety.

Contact
Email: pen.e.fund@gmail.com

_ ICORN

ICORN is an independent organisation of cities and regions offering shelter
to writers and artists who are at risk for advancing freedom of expression,
defending democratic values and promoting international solidarity.
The original *Cities of Asylum Network* (INCA) was founded in 1993 by the
International Parliament of Writers (IPW) in response to the assassination of
writers in Algeria. Salman Rushdie, Wole Soyinka and Vaclav Havel were
presidents. Council members included J.M. Coetzee, Jacques Derrida,
Margaret Drabble, and Harold Pinter. The idea to create a network of cities
to shelter threatened writers was first embraced by Barcelona and quickly
followed by many others, including cities in the United States and Mexico.
The IPW was dissolved in 2005, but the scheme was left intact.

In 2010, ICORN became an independent membership organisation
and in 2014 the ICORN general assembly voted to expand the scope of
writers and offer residencies for artists and musicians.

Writers and artists are especially vulnerable to censorship,
harassment, imprisonment and even death, because of what they do. They
represent the liberating gift of the human imagination and give voice to
thoughts, ideas, debate and critique, disseminated to a wide audience.
They also tend to be the first to speak out and resist when free speech is
threatened.

ICORN member-cities offer long term, but temporary, shelter to
those at risk as a direct consequence of their creative activities. ICORN's aim
is to host as many persecuted writers and artists as possible in ICORN cities
and, together with its sister networks, to form a dynamic and sustainable
global network for freedom of expression.

ICORN is both a literature/arts *and* a human rights/freedom of
expression organisation. Culturally, it interacts with local initiatives in the
member cities, national arts councils, and internationally with a wide range

of arts and literature festivals, residency networks, and so on.

ICORN protects and promotes an increasingly wide range of writers, artists and human rights defenders, including bloggers, novelists, playwrights, journalists, musicians, poets, non-fiction writers, visual artists, cartoonists, singer/songwriters, translators, screenwriters and publishers. ICORN enables them to continue to express themselves freely in a place where they are safe, but not silent. Through digital media, they can reach audiences to which they were denied access before leaving. And through local and ICORN networks, their voices can also be heard by new audiences in their host cities and beyond.

Since 2006, more than 50 cities around the globe have joined the network, and no less than 130 writers and artists have found shelter in an ICORN member city. The commitment by these cities is both concrete and symbolic: the agent for change (the writer/artist) escapes from imminent threat and persecution; the host city offers sanctuary, and the values of hospitality, solidarity, and freedom of expression become further enshrined in the ethos of that city.

The ICORN Administration Center was established in Stavanger in June 2006 at the Stavanger Cultural Center, Sølvberget. It works closely with PEN International and its Writers in Prison Committee, which evaluates the authenticity of authorship and artistic production as well as declared danger. ICORN depends heavily on cooperation with PEN International, Article 19, Reporters without Borders, and others. Since 2010, ICORN has been involved in relevant projects in the European Parliament and the European Commission and particularly with the EU's initiative to set up a global system of shelter for those who defend human rights.

Contact
c/o Sølvberget KF
Stavanger Cultural Centre
P.O.Box 310
4002 Stavanger
Norway
Email: icorn@icorn.org

_ Eva Tas Foundation

The Eva Tas Foundation (ETF) encourages publication and promotion of texts that are, no matter where and how, subject to censorship. A world in which people, in any context, can write about what they believe and read whatever they wish. That was the dream of the Dutch teacher and journalist Eva Tas. This was the spirit in which she spent her life opposing all forms of censorship and decided to devote her estate to defending the freedom of the written word.

The foundation aims, without the pursuit of profit, to stand up for the freedom of the written word and to propagate, nationally, and internationally, the importance and meaning of this. The foundation strives to achieve this by opposing any form of repression with regard to the freedom of the written word, particularly by (i) supporting the publication and promotion of texts being threatened with censorship, (ii) in incidental cases, part-subsidizing the publication of books of exiled journalists and writers, and (iii) participating in common initiatives and activities. [46]

The ETF carries out this task in various ways by granting financial support to the publication of books in ETF's *Censorship Series* by writers who – as noted – no matter where or how, are being impeded in the practice of their profession.

Contact
Eva Tas Foundation
Mail: rudolfgeel@evatasfoundation.com

_ Amnesty International

In 1961, British lawyer Peter Benenson was outraged when two Portuguese students were jailed just for raising a toast to freedom. He wrote an article in *The Observer* newspaper and launched a campaign that provoked an incredible response. Reprinted in newspapers across the world, his call to action sparked the idea that people everywhere can unite in solidarity for justice and freedom. This inspiring moment didn't just give birth to an extraordinary

---

46 An example of ETF's partly subsidizing books is *Delayed Democracy; How Press Freedom Collapsed in The Gambia*, written by Alagi Yorro Jallow. Published in 2103 by Author House

movement; it was the start of extraordinary social change.

Only when the last prisoner of conscience has been freed, when the last torture chamber has been closed, when the United Nations Universal Declaration of Human Rights is a reality for the world's people, will Amnesty's work be done.

Governments pay lip service to 'free speech' in almost every constitution in the world, but the reality isn't so free. Across the world people are thrown into prison for speaking out.

People's right to seek, receive, and share information and ideas without fear or unlawful interference, is crucial for their education to develop as individuals, help communities, access justice, and enjoy all other human rights.

Since Amnesty began, it supported and protected people who speak out – for themselves and for others. It works with journalists, community workers and teachers, trade unionists, people promoting reproductive rights and indigenous people standing up for their land rights.

Amnesty has campaigned all round the world for thousands of prisoners of conscience – those who have not used or advocated violence but is imprisoned because of who they are (sexual orientation, ethnic, national or social origin, language, birth, colour, sex or economic status) or what they believe in (religious, political or other conscientiously held beliefs). Governments often use 'national security' as a reason to stifle criticism. In recent years, terrorism has helped justify increased repression.

Blogger Raif Badawi is serving a 10-year prison sentence in Saudi Arabia, for setting up a website for social and political debate. Another local blogger explains: "They seek to gag and stifle dissent using various means, including the shameful Terrorism Law that has become a sword waved in the face of people with opinions. Courts issue prison sentences of 10 years or more because of a single tweet. Atheists and people who contact human rights organizations are attacked as 'terrorists'."

Journalists
Amnesty calls for:

- Prisoners of conscience around the world to be released immediately without any conditions attached.
- All laws criminalizing people who speak out, or protest peacefully, to be struck off the law books.
- Laws against hate speech or other incitements to violence not to be used to repress valid dissent.
- People to have access to information.

Expression, association and assembly
Freedom of expression is closely related to freedom of association and peaceful assembly.

Freedom of association – having the right to meet with anyone you choose, such as to form and join clubs, societies or trade unions to pursue your interests. *Freedom of peaceful assembly* – having the right to take part in a peaceful assembly, such as a demonstration or public meeting.

Digital frontier
The digital world levels the playing field and gives many more of us access to the information we need to challenge governments and corporations. Information is power and the internet has the potential to significantly empower the world's seven billion people giving all of us the means to express what we see and feel, wherever we are and whatever we witness. Increasingly states try to build firewalls around digital communications. Iran, China, and Viet Nam have all tried to develop systems to control access to digital information. In India's northern Kashmir region, mobile Internet and communications are suspended in response to any unrest. In 2014, Amnesty and a coalition of human rights and technology organisations launched 'Detekt' – a simple tool that allows activists to scan their devices for surveillance spyware.

Over the years, human rights have moved from the fringes to centre stage in world affairs. Amnesty has grown from seeking the release of political prisoners to upholding the whole spectrum of human rights.

Amnesty's work protects and empowers people – from abolishing the death penalty to protecting sexual and reproductive rights, and from combating discrimination to defending refugees and migrants' rights. Amnesty speaks out for anyone whose freedom and dignity are under threat.

Contact
Amnesty International
Address: 1 Easton Street,
London, WC1X 0DW,
United Kingdom
Email: contactus@amnesty.org
Telephone: +44-20-74135500
Twitter:@Amnestyonline

_ Prisoners of Conscience

Originally established in 1962 as the relief arm of Amnesty International, Prisoners of Conscience (PoC) is a separate charity and the only agency in the UK making grants specifically to prisoners of conscience – individuals who have been persecuted for their conscientiously-held beliefs, provided that they have not used or advocated violence. PoC's grant recipients include political prisoners, human rights defenders, lawyers, environmental activists, teachers, and academics who come from many different countries such as Burma, Zimbabwe, Sri Lanka, Tibet, Iran, Cameroon and Eritrea. PoC's aim is to raise and distribute money to help prisoners of conscience and/or their families to rehabilitate themselves during and after their ordeal. Financial grants cover general hardship relief, furniture, medicines, travel costs, family reunion costs, education, requalification and resettlement costs and medical treatment and counseling after torture.

PoC runs a small office, with one full-time and two part-time staff members, and a team of dedicated volunteers.

Applications for relief and bursary grants are submitted by approved referral agencies. Detailed application forms are completed by the referral agency on behalf of the applicant. The application is then considered by a sub-committee of trustees of PoC, with advice from the office. It takes three to four weeks from the moment that the application is received to the receipt of the cheque by the referral agency.

PoC provides two types of financial assistance to prisoners of conscience:
1. Relief and rehabilitation grants (which could include family reunions)
2. Bursary grants for post graduate study

Relief Grants

PoC is the only agency in the UK making grants specifically to individual prisoners of conscience both in exile in the UK and overseas. PoC co-operates with over 50 different referral agencies such as human rights organisations, refugee groups, community organisations, colleges or solicitors to distribute relief funds to beneficiaries.

PoC grants are modest – up to £350 per person – and cover life-sustaining items such as food, clothing, furniture, non-prescription drugs etc. Other grants cover medical treatment, travel costs, family reunion costs, education, counseling and rehabilitation for torture survivors, requalification costs and resettlement costs.

Bursary Grants

Bursary grants are much larger than the normal relief grants, and were funded initially with the help of a generous legacy. Since then, several ongoing donations from individuals and charitable trusts have allowed the programme to be continued.

The recipients of PoC's grants are people who have been persecuted for their conscientiously-held beliefs. They are people who have stood up for what they believe is right, usually in terrifying circumstances and often with the knowledge that their actions would open themselves and their families up to terrible danger. PoC will not help anyone who has used or condoned violence.

PoC's aim is to help as many people as possible with the funds available; people in considerable distress whose lives have been destroyed by persecution.

Contact
The Prisoners of Conscience Appeal Fund
po box 61044
SE1 1UP
London
United Kingdom
Telephone: +44 (0) 20 7407 6644
Fax: +44 (0) 20 7407 6655
E-mail: info@prisonersofconscience.org

_ Human Rights Watch

Human Rights Watch (HRW) defends the rights of people worldwide. HRW scrupulously investigates abuses, exposes the facts widely, and pressures those with power to respect rights and secure justice. HRW is an independent, international organisation that works as part of a movement to uphold human dignity and advance the cause of human rights for all. Its work is guided by international human rights and humanitarian law and respect for the dignity of each human being.

HRW is a nonprofit, nongovernmental human rights organisation made up of roughly 400 staff members around the globe. Its staff consists of human rights professionals, including country experts, lawyers, journalists, and academics of diverse backgrounds and nationalities.

To ensure HRW's independence, it does not accept government funds, directly or indirectly, or support from any private funder that could compromise its objectivity and independence.

Established in 1978, HRW is known for its accurate fact-finding, impartial reporting, effective use of media, and targeted advocacy, often in partnership with local human rights groups. Each year, it publishes more than 100 reports and briefings on human rights conditions in some 90 countries, generating extensive coverage in local and international media. This leverage gives it access to governments, the UN, regional bodies like the African Union and the European Union, financial institutions, and corporations to press for changes in policy and practices that promote human rights and justice around the world.

HRW works closely with a broad range of local and international civil society actors, researchers, and journalists to maximize its impact. HRW speaks out against attacks on freedom of the media, on civil society, and defends the political space within which the broader human rights movement operates.

Two researchers, F. Makki and C. Geisler, analyzed a land-eviction case in the Gambella Region, Ethiopia. This is what exiled Ethiopian journalist Handiso wrote about HRW's support in the case: 'In preparation of the influx of foreign investors, peasants and pastoralists were evicted or transferred to other places. One example concerns the semi-nomadic Nuer people: they were forcibly transferred to Bildak, a new village in the Gambella Region. The Nuer quickly abandoned Bildak in May 2011 because there was no water source for their cattle.... The case was taken up by the Bank's independent Inspection Panel, which concluded that the Bank indeed violated its own policies in Ethiopia (the World Bank was involved in developing the area, PdH) Jessica Evans, *Human Rights Watch's* senior financial institutions researcher, concluded that the Inspection Panel's report showed that the World Bank had largely ignored human rights risks evident in its projects in Ethiopia. The Bank now has the opportunity and responsibility to adjust course on its Ethiopia programming and to provide redress to those who were harmed. But management's Action Plan achieves neither, according to Evans'. From: *Genocide of Thought*, p. 30.

HRW documents right abuses around the world with the ultimate goal of ending them and bringing the perpetrators to justice. Change doesn't come easily. And it rarely comes from HRW's efforts alone, but rather from the combined efforts of numerous groups and activists. Progress can take many forms – laws are changed, investigations launched, international pressure is applied, perpetrators brought before courts – but each is a step forward in the pursuit of justice, the promotion of human rights, and freedom of expression. HRW's website, under the heading 'Impact', includes recent reports of successful HRW interventions.

Contact
Human Rights Watch
350 Fifth Avenue, 34th floor
New York, NY 10118-3299
USA
No email address provided.
Tel:+1-212-290-4700

_ The Open Society Foundations

The Open Society Foundations work to build vibrant and tolerant societies whose governments are accountable and open to the participation of all people. They seek to strengthen the rule of law; respect for human rights, minorities, and a diversity of opinions; democratically elected governments; and a civil society that helps keep government power in check.
The Open Society Foundations help to shape public policies that assure greater fairness in political, legal, and economic systems and safeguard fundamental rights. They implement initiatives to advance independent media, justice, education, and public health. They build alliances across borders and continents on issues such as corruption and freedom of information.

Working in every part of the world, the Open Society Foundations place a high priority on protecting and improving the lives of people in marginalized communities.

The Open Society Foundations began in 1979 when George Soros decided he had enough money. His great success as a hedge fund manager allowed him to pursue his ambition of establishing open societies in place of authoritarian forms of government. "Open society is based on the recognition that our understanding of the world is inherently imperfect," Soros said. "What is imperfect can be improved." He started by supporting scholarships for black students at the University of Cape Town in South Africa and for Eastern European dissidents to study abroad.

Soros set up his first non-U.S. foundation in Hungary in 1984. It distributed photocopiers to universities, libraries, and civil society groups, breaking the communist party's grip on information. When the Berlin Wall fell, Soros had already established two more foundations, one in Poland and the other in Russia. As communism collapsed, he moved quickly to create foundations in countries throughout Eastern Europe and Central Asia. His work contributed to the emergence of democratic governments and substantially more open societies in most countries of the former Soviet empire.

Aryeh Neier, Soros's successor, made the Open Society Foundations into a truly international organisation. They provided support for Burmese refugees and dissidents suffering under the repressive military regime; for the construction of low-cost housing and legal, economic, and political reforms in South Africa to help the fledgling majority black government; and for regional initiatives in Africa and Central Asia. In 1996, with the launch of its programs in the United States, Open Society made an effort to address some of the flaws of an open society. Its geographical reach continued to expand in the first decade of the new millennium. By 2010 it played a role in every region of the world.

The Open Society Program on Independent Journalism seeks to promote independent and viable media and professional, quality journalism in countries undergoing a process of democratization, and building functioning media markets. The program sees independent journalism as playing a crucial role in the functioning of democracies and in establishing standards for practices and content in a media environment marked by evolving communications technologies.

Assistance to Media Outlets
The Program on Independent Journalism provides assistance to media outlets that promote democratic values and demonstrate, through their editorial approach, a high level of professionalism, independence, and openness.

Journalism and Media Management Training
Open Society supports training aimed at current or future media professionals, including instruction in professional skills and in-depth reporting on specialized areas such as human rights, minorities, economics and finance, education, public health, and elections.

Media Self-Regulation and Accountability
The program supports development of appropriate mechanisms for ensuring increased professionalism, accuracy, and adherence to ethical standards among journalists.

Media-Related Research
The program supports research as the basis for subsequent activities in policymaking, advocacy, and training.

Media Association Building
This program includes support for the development of professional membership-based associations, including through partnerships with appropriate international bodies and umbrella institutions.

Promotion of Media Freedom
This program promotes media freedom by supporting projects that ensure monitoring and defence of journalists' rights and that advocate an open legal and regulatory environment.

Contact
Open Society Foundation
7th Floor, Millbank Tower, 21–24 Millbank
London SW1P 4QP
United Kingdom
Phone: +44-207-031-0200
Fax: +44-207-031-0201

CHAPTER IV
A BRIGHTER FUTURE?

Will censorship prevail; will censorship continue to overtake freedom of expression and freedom of the media? This essay's story suggests that this may not necessarily be the case. After all, the current period – in which censorship is on the rise again – was preceded by a period in which censorship was diminishing. Depending on future political developments it is possible that we will experience another wave of democratisation during which freedom of expression may flourish again. This is the political dimension of freedom and censorship.

There is an *economic* dimension to censorship and freedom of expression as well. Authoritarian governments that apply censorship can claim that at best they promote economic growth, and at worst that they don't put a break on growth. This is what the regression analyses presented in chapter II suggest. However, the good news is that they also tell us that the more a country invests in its economic development, the greater the chance that freedom of the press improves.

There is another hopeful development going on triggered by the internet, through social network sites such as Facebook, Twitter, and the like. These communication channels are being used by a rapidly increasing number of citizen journalists, who report events in places from which professional reporters are banned. True, the authorities try to shut down these channels, but it may well be that shutting them down will become more and more difficult for them.

The large majority of Partly Free and Not Free countries are developing countries. Most of them have received development aid over the past 60 years. This aid has apparently not been effective in promoting economic development and, related to it, in helping to create *open societies* in Popper's sense. Part of the blame goes to aid-receiving governments that have been unwilling – or incapable – to bring about development. These governments haven't been eager to promote freedom of the media, as the media would certainly have exposed the political leadership's failures. Another part of the blame has to go to aid givers who failed in helping countries to move from Not Free or Partly Free to Free countries.

Countries – and cities in particular – which offer a rich variety in music, ballet, literature, museums, exhibitions, festivals, bookshops, what have you, contribute to the 'good life' of individuals. Writers play an important part in enriching the cultural climate in society. Culture at large also contributes to a country's economic development through its inspirational strength in the realm of innovation and in broadening society's understanding of complex political and economic issues.

No one knows whether the present increase in censorship will further spread across the world. There are many yet unknown factors that may result in more or less censorship. A current question is whether, for example, the attacks of Islamic State and affiliated religious extremist groups will negatively impinge upon the liberal values defended by the organisations mentioned in chapter III and by countries adhering to the same values of democracy and freedom.

There is one thing we know and that is that without all the organisations that defend freedom of expression, and protect journalists, bloggers, writers, and publishers who oppose censorship, censorship will not be challenged.

Given the current growing threats to freedom, it is essential that all organisations dedicated to defending freedom of expression and freedom of the media must be heard loud and clear. They must strive for full cooperation with each other to enhance their impact in every country where censorship is a common phenomenon.

Annexe I Freedom House's methodology

FH's examination of the level of press freedom in each country is based on 23 methodology questions divided into three broad categories: the legal environment, the political environment, and the economic environment. For each methodology question, a lower number of points is allotted for a more free situation, while a higher number of points is allotted for a less free environment. Each country is rated in these three categories, with the higher numbers indicating less freedom. A country's final score is based on the total of the three categories: A score of 0 to 30 places the country in the Free press group; 31 to 60 in the Partly Free press group; and 61 to 100 in the Not Free press group.

The diverse nature of the methodology questions seeks to encompass the varied ways in which pressure can be placed upon the flow of information and the ability of print, broadcast, and internet-based media to operate freely and without fear of repercussions: In short, FH seeks to provide a picture of the entire "enabling environment" in which the media in each country operate. FH also seeks to assess the degree of news and information diversity available to the public in any given country, from either local or transnational sources.

The **legal environment** category encompasses an examination of both the laws and regulations that could influence media content and the government's inclination to use these laws and legal institutions to restrict the media's ability to operate. FH assesses the positive impact of legal and constitutional guarantees for freedom of expression; the potentially negative aspects of security legislation, the penal code, and other criminal statutes; penalties for libel and defamation; the existence of, and ability to, use freedom of information legislation; the independence of the judiciary and of official media regulatory bodies; registration requirements for both media outlets and journalists; and the ability of journalists' groups to operate freely.

Under the **political environment** category, FH evaluates the degree of political control over the content of news media. Issues examined include the editorial independence of both state-owned and privately owned media;

access to information and sources; official censorship and self-censorship; the vibrancy of the media and the diversity of news available within each country; the ability of both foreign and local reporters to cover the news freely and without harassment; and the intimidation of journalists by the state or other actors, including arbitrary detention and imprisonment, violent assaults, and other threats.

FH's third category examines the **economic environment** for the media. This includes the structure of media ownership; transparency and concentration of ownership; the costs of establishing media as well as of production and distribution; the selective withholding of advertising or subsidies by the state or other actors; the impact of corruption and bribery on content; and the extent to which the economic situation in a country impacts the development and sustainability of the media.

Annexe II Dot plots and statistical details

Dot plots including all countries with HDI and Economic Growth

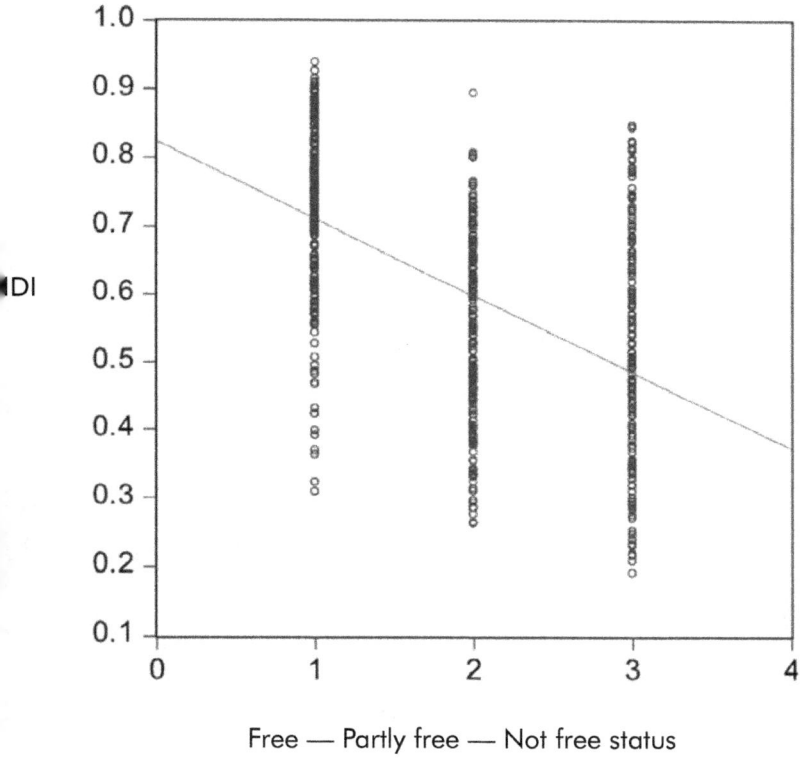

Free — Partly free — Not free status

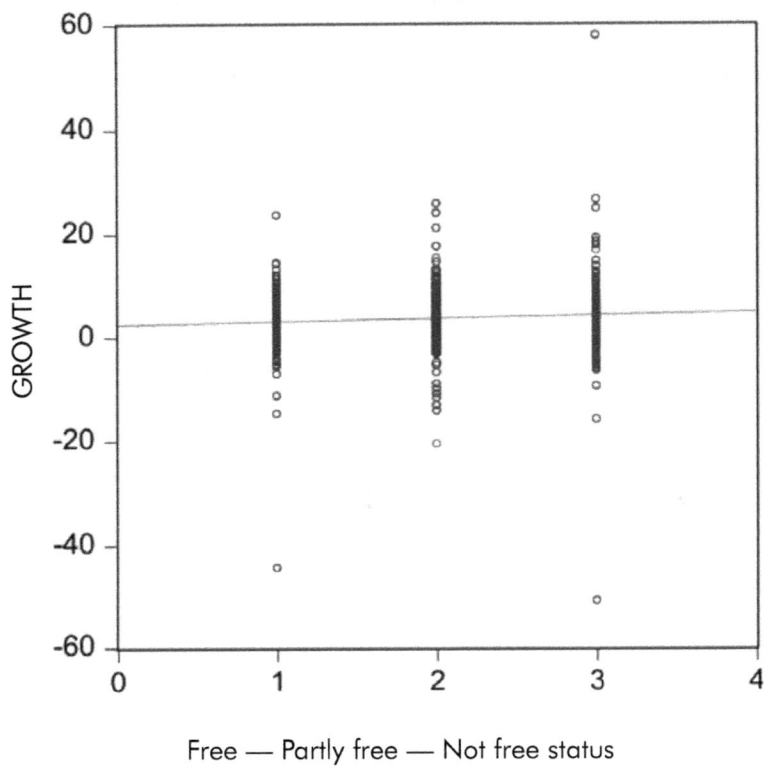

GROWTH

Free — Partly free — Not free status

Dot plots excluding outliers (countries with economic growth of more than 15% or less than minus 15% are excluded)

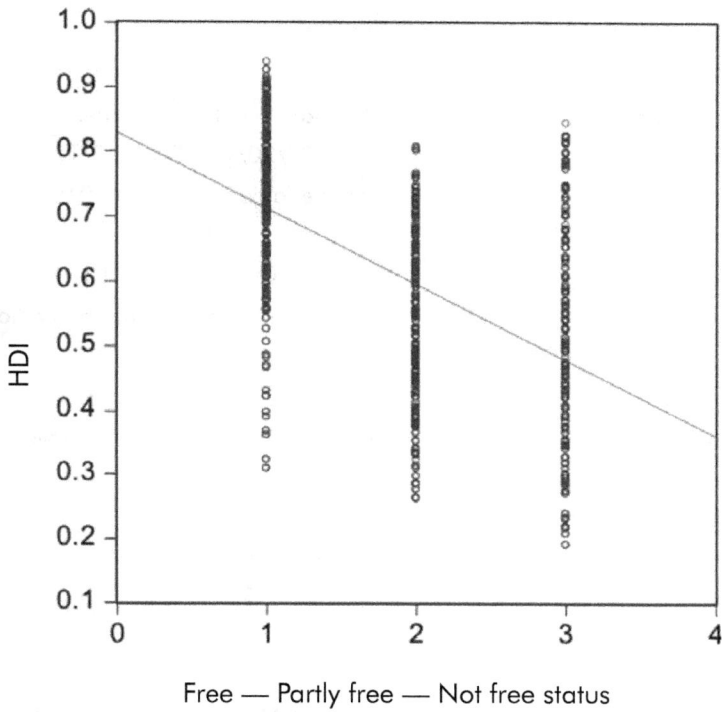

Free — Partly free — Not free status

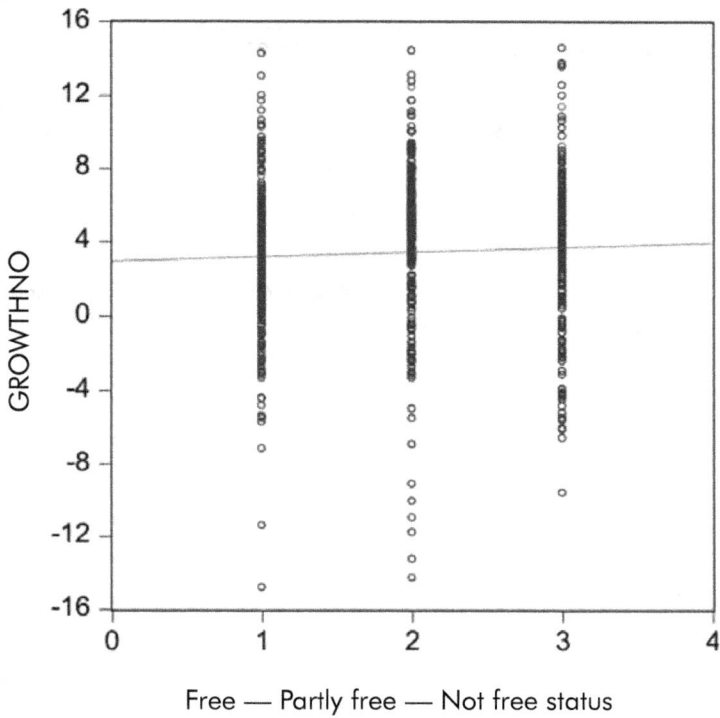

Free — Partly free — Not free status

85

All Countries

Dependent Variable: HDI
Method: Panel Least Squares
Date: 07/20/15   Time: 17:17
Sample (adjusted): 1980 2010
Periods included: 4
Cross-sections included: 181
Total panel (unbalanced) observations: 543

Dependent Variable: GROWTH
Method: Panel Least Squares
Date: 07/20/15   Time: 17:17
Sample (adjusted): 1980 2010
Periods included: 4
Cross-sections included: 181
Total panel (unbalanced) observations:

Variable	Coefficient	Std, Error	t-Statistic	Prob,
C	0,82	0,02	51,73	0,00
STATUS	-0,12	0,01	-14,50	0,00
GROWTH	0,00	0,00	1,13	0,26

Variable	Coefficient	Std, Error	t-Statistic	Pro
C	0,69	1,42	0,49	0,6
STATUS	1,19	0,34	3,49	0,0
HDI	1,78	1,57	1,13	0,2

R-squared	0,28	Mean dependent var	0,62
Adjusted R-squared	0,28	S,D, dependent var	0,17
S,E, of regression	0,15	Akaike info criterion	-0,99
Sum squared resid	11,66	Schwarz criterion	-0,97
Log likelihood	272,26	Hannan-Quinn criter,	-0,98
F-statistic	105,66	Durbin-Watson stat	0,31
Prob (F-statistic)	0,00		

R-squared	0,02	Mean dependent var	3,9
Adjusted R-squared	0,02	S,D, dependent var	5,4
S,E, of regression	5,38	Akaike info criterion	6,2
Sum squared resid	15635,22	Schwarz criterion	6,2
Log likelihood	-1682,77	Hannan-Quinn criter,	6,2
F-statistic	6,44	Durbin-Watson stat	1,6
Prob (F-statistic)	0,00		

xcluding Outliers

Dependent Variable: HDI	Dependent Variable: GROWTHNO
Method: Panel Least Squares	Method: Panel Least Squares
Date: 07/20/15 Time: 17:18	Date: 07/20/15 Time: 17:18
Sample (adjusted): 1980 2010	Sample (adjusted): 1980 2010
Periods included: 4	Periods included: 4
Cross-sections included: 180	Cross-sections included: 180
Total panel (unbalanced) observations: 529	Total panel (unbalanced) observations: 529

Variable	Coefficient	Std, Error	t-Statistic	Prob,
C	0,82	0,02	50,56	0,00
STATUS	-0,12	0,01	-14,66	0,00
GROWTHNO	0,00	0,00	1,30	0,19

R-squared	0,29	Mean dependent var	0,62
Adjusted R-squared	0,29	S,D, dependent var	0,17
S,E, of regression	0,15	Akaike info criterion	-1,00
Sum squared resid	11,24	Schwarz criterion	-0,98
Log likelihood	268,16	Hannan-Quinn criter,	-0,99
F-statistic	107,44	Durbin-Watson stat	0,31
Prob (F-statistic)	0,00		

Variable	Coefficient	Std, Error	t-Statistic	Prob,
C	1,39	1,14	1,22	0,22
STATUS	0,65	0,27	2,37	0,02
HDI	1,64	1,26	1,30	0,19

R-squared	0,01	Mean dependent var	3,58
Adjusted R-squared	0,01	S,D, dependent var	4,25
S,E, of regression	4,23	Akaike info criterion	5,73
Sum squared resid	9419,89	Schwarz criterion	5,75
Log likelihood	-1512,27	Hannan-Quinn criter,	5,74
F-statistic	2,82	Durbin-Watson stat	1,70
Prob (F-statistic)	0,06		

The graphs depicting the *reverse relationships*

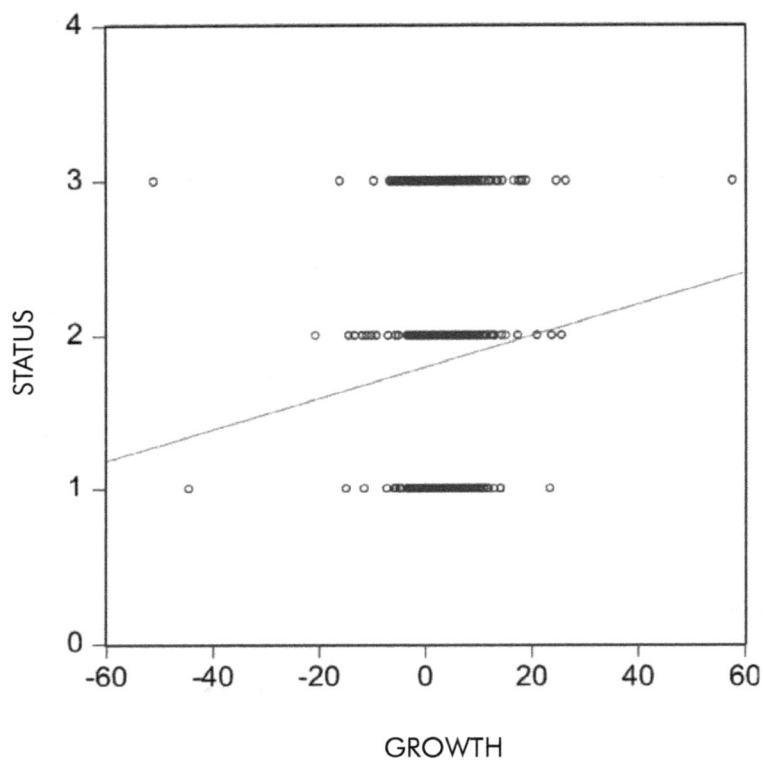

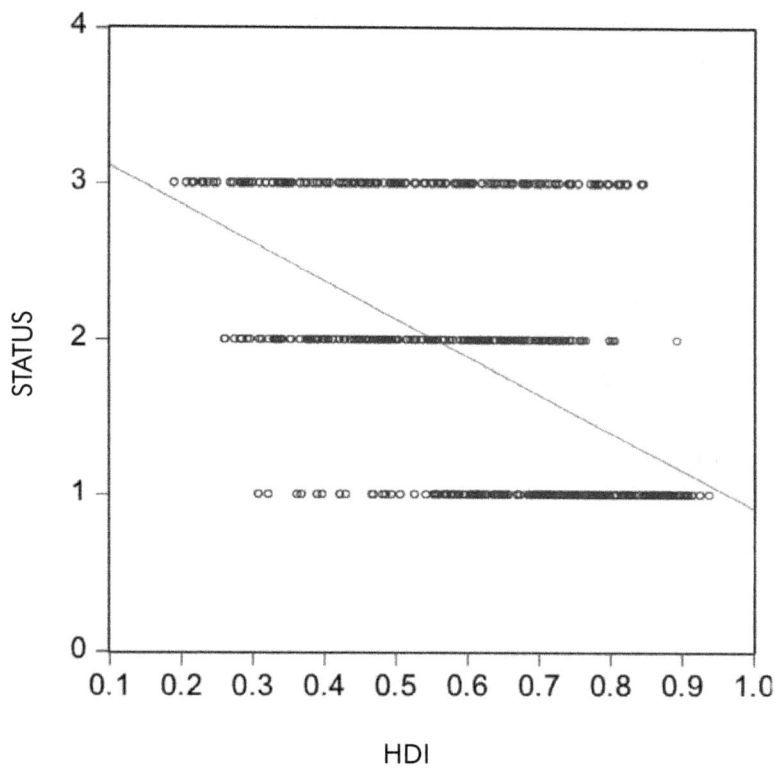

Regression All Countries

Dependent Variable: STATUS
Method: Panel Least Squares
Date: 09/02/15   Time: 14:58
Sample (adjusted): 1980 2010
Periods included: 4
Cross-sections included: 181
Total panel (unbalanced) observations: 543

Variable	Coefficient	Std, Error	t-Statistic	Prob,
C	3,25	0,11	29,54	0,00
HDI	-2,42	0,17	-14,50	0,00
GROWTH	0,02	0,01	3,49	0,00

R-squared	0,30	Mean dependent var	1,82
Adjusted R-squared	0,29	S,D, dependent var	0,80
S,E, of regression	0,67	Akaike info criterion	2,05
Sum squared resid	244,50	Schwarz criterion	2,07
Log likelihood	-553,85	Hannan-Quinn criter,	2,06
F-statistic	113,23	Durbin-Watson stat	0,65
Prob (F-statistic)	0,00		

Regression No Outliers

Dependent Variable: STATUS
Method: Panel Least Squares
Date: 09/02/15   Time: 15:17
Sample (adjusted): 1980 2010
Periods included: 4
Cross-sections included: 180
Total panel (unbalanced) observations: 5

Variable	Coefficient	Std, Error	t-Statistic	Prob
C	3,28	0,11	29,52	0,00
HDI	-2,47	0,17	-14,66	0,00
GROWTHNO	0,02	0,01	2,37	0,02

R-squared	0,30	Mean dependent var	1,8
Adjusted R-squared	0,29	S,D, dependent var	0,80
S,E, of regression	0,67	Akaike info criterion	2,05
Sum squared resid	237,01	Schwarz criterion	2,07
Log likelihood	-538,26	Hannan-Quinn criter,	2,06
F-statistic	110,21	Durbin-Watson stat	0,64
Prob (F-statistic)	0,00		

Bibliography

Acemoglu, D., Naidu, S., Restrepo, P., Robinson, J. (1 May 2015). *Democracy Does Cause Growth.*

Alam, A., Shah, S.Z. (2013) The Role of Press Freedom in Economic Development; A Global Perspective; *Journal of Media Economics*, Vol. 26, Issue 1

Berendsen, B. Ed. (2010) *Economic Growth and the Common Good.* Amsterdam: KIT Publishers.

Berger, P. (1987) *The Capitalist Revolution; Fifty Propositions about Prosperity, Equality, &Liberty.* Aldershot: Gower Press.

Carothers, T. (2008) Does Democracy Promotion Have a Future? *Democracy and Development.* Amsterdam: KIT Publishers

Committee to Protect Journalists (2006, 2015) *Ten Most Censored Countries.* New York: CPJ website.

Daly, E. (2014) *We Need Journalism.* Esglbal.org

Easterly, W. (2008) Freedom and Development. *Democracy and Development.* Amsterdam: KIT Publishers.

Fase, M. M. G. (2002) *Het economisch gedachtengoed van Pieter Hennipman (1911-1994)*

Freedom House *Global Press Freedom Report 2007.* Washington, DC: Freedom House website.

Freedom House *Global Press Freedom Report 2015.* Washington, DC: Freedom House website.

Friedman, M. (2002) *Capitalism and Freedom;* 40th anniversary edition. Chicago: Chicago University Press.

French, H. W. (2014) *China's Second Continent.* New York: Knopf.

Handiso, B.W. (2015) *Genocide of the Mind.* Amsterdam: Eva Tas Foundation.

Hayek, F. A. 1960 *The Constitution of Liberty.* London: Routledge.

Hennipman, P. (1945) *Economisch Motief en Economisch Principe.* Amsterdam: N.V. Noord-Hollandse Uitgevers Maatschappij.

Human Rights Watch, website.

Ibrahim, A. (2008) Democracy and Islam. *Democracy and Development.* Amsterdam: KIT Publishers.

Judt, T. (1998) Albert Camus: The Reluctant Moralist. *The Burden of Responsibility.* Chicago: Chicago University Press.

Meza, D. (2015) *Kidnapped.* Amsterdam: Eva Tas Foundation

Popper, K. R.*The Open Society and its Enemies.* Vol. I. London: Routledge & Kegan Paul

Orwell, G. (1984) Inside the Whale. *The Penguin Essays of George Orwell.* Harmondsworth: Penguin Books.

Orwell, G. (1984) The Prevention of Literature. *The Penguin Essays of George Orwell.* Harmondsworth: Penguin Books.

Schumpeter, J.A. (1970) *Capitalism, Socialism and Democracy.* London: Unwin University Books.

Scitovsky, T. (1992) *The Joyless Economy; the Psychology of Human Satisfaction.* New York: Oxford University Press.

Sun, S. (2015) *Drugs for the Mind.* Amsterdam: Eva Tas Foundation.

UNDP (2007, 2015) *Human Development Report.* New York: UNDP website.

UNESCO (2008) *Press Freedom and Development.* Paris: UNESCO website.

Van der Ploeg, R. (2002) In Art We Trust. De Economist, Vol. 150, No.4.

Von Vegesack, T. (1989). *De Intellectuelen; een Geschiedenis van het Literaire Engagement 1898-1968.* Amsterdam: Meulenhoff.

World Bank. *World Development Indicators.* Washington, D.C.: World Bank website.

PREVIOUSLY APPEARED IN THE SERIES

_ Honduras _ Dina Meza, *Kidnapped*
_ Vietnam _ Bui Thanh Hieu, *Speaking in Silence*
_ China _ Sofie Sun, *Drugs for the Mind*
_ Ethiopia _ Bisrat Handiso, *Genocide of Thought*
_ Macedonia _ Tomislav Kezharovski, *Likvidacija/Annihilation*

To appear this spring:
_ Cuba _ Amir Valle, *Gagged*
_ Bangladesh _ MD **Parvez Alam**, *Disappearing Public-Spheres*
_ Turkey _ Fréderike Geerdink, *Bans, Jails and Shameless Lies*

To appear in autumn:
_ El Salvador _ Jorge Galán, *The Long Shadow*
_ Suriname _ Sylvana van den Braak, *A Fri Wortu*

If in stock the printed titles are available for free via:
Janhonout@evatasfoundation.com.
Available as an ebook via the common outlets.

www.ingramcontent.com/pod-product-compliance
Lightning Source LLC
Chambersburg PA
CBHW060514280326
41933CB00014B/2961